STAY HUNGRY.
STAY FOOLISH.

STAY HUNGRY.
STAY FOOLISH.

Advice for the Rest of Your Life –
Classic Graduation Speeches

WH
ALLEN

1 3 5 7 9 10 8 6 4 2

WH Allen, an imprint of Ebury Publishing,
20 Vauxhall Bridge Road,
London SW1V 2SA

WH Allen is part of the Penguin Random House group of companies
whose addresses can be found at global.penguinrandomhouse.com

Penguin
Random House
UK

First published in the United Kingdom by WH Allen in 2019

www.penguin.co.uk

A CIP catalogue record for this book is available from the British Library

Hardback ISBN 9780753553503

Typeset in 10.75/16.8 pts Sabon LT Std
by Integra Software Services Pvt. Ltd, Pondicherry

Printed and bound in Great Britain by Clays Ltd, Elcograf S.p.A.

Penguin Random House is committed to a sustainable future for
our business, our readers and our planet. This book is made
from Forest Stewardship Council® certified paper.

CONTENTS

MERYL STREEP

OPENING THE DOOR

University of New Hampshire, 2003

Good morning, Governor Benson, President Hart, members of the Board of Trustees, distinguished faculty, proud parents and you, almost alumni. I'm very pleased to be here today to address you on this day, your last day of wearing your tassels on the left. I have agonized over this speech, mostly because I don't usually give speeches, or when I do, it's at my house, and nobody listens. I have thought long and hard about how to advise you, inspire you, thrill and excite you over multiple speakers that repeat each word-erd-erd in that sonic-onic-onic Doppler-oppler-oppler effect-ect-ect that makes you want to go to sleep-eep-eep. Meryl Streep-eep-eep put me to sleep-eep-eep. Probably quite a few of you need a great deal of sleep after all of the parties, er, studying, finals and things of Senior Spring. And if you're at all like my college-age children, you're used to getting most of your sleep during daylight hours ... am I right?

Because I want you not to doze, I decided I should avoid politics. Also, of course, I am in show business, and not allowed to speak about politics. Or, I'm allowed to speak, of course I'm allowed to speak, and never work again.

But my problem is: I've never heard of anybody making anything but a political speech in New Hampshire. Nobody makes a speech in New Hampshire unless they're stumping for something, do they? I think it's a state law, isn't it? Your honour? If I have to, by law, make a political speech, you'll sleep. But if I make a speech about sex, you'll wake up. See, it's already working! So I'll make a speech about sexual politics, and I won't be running for anything except, perhaps, cover.

I went to school in New Hampshire 30 years ago as one of the first women to integrate Dartmouth College. We were 60 intrepid girls on a campus of approximately 6,000 men. We tried to lead them, gently, towards a difficult idea (one that UNH has endorsed almost since its inception): the idea that women are valuable to a university. It was not as difficult as convincing the Taliban more recently of the same thing, but I do remember some pitched battles back then. Your graduation class today of nearly 3,000 students is almost 2-to-1 women, and your school is not an anomaly. This imbalance, to differing degrees, is replicated at colleges and universities around the country. In the huge University of California system, women are in a strong majority, averaging around 57 per cent of the student population. According to *Peterson's Guide*, at NYU and Boston University, the percentage is 60–40 women to men. What's going on? And who, 30 years ago, would've ever predicted it? (Maybe the Taliban had a legitimate fear: give them an inch and they'll just take over!)

These statistics are all the more confusing when we acknowledge the fact that the glass ceiling is still in effect in the business world, the professions and politics. Imagine if the Senate were apportioned in the same way as your graduating class! Or that there were twice as many women as men in the House!? Or the White House! Or on cable news!? At the heads of Fortune 500 companies? It's almost unimaginable. You can scan the mastheads of major news organizations, the lists of the top echelons of business and management, the hierarchies of power in government, and it still reads pretty much like it did in the middle of the last century, or the century before that, or the centuries before that. In other words, it's like the membership list of the Augusta Golf Club today.

Why is there this discrepancy between how many women succeed in college and where they actually end up? What happens to all these people after graduation? Back in 1970 we thought that if we had access to the same educational opportunities as men, then the same opportunities would naturally present themselves out in the real world. We've more than crashed through the first, the educational barrier, but the other is proving tougher to go up against. It may seem as if universities are optimistically and successfully preparing an unprecedented number of female students for leadership opportunities

Guard your good mood. Listen to music every day, joke, and love and read more for fun, especially poetry.

that don't exist. Many women will confront the attitude of top PGA golfer Vijay Singh when he declared he would rather quit the tournament than play alongside the top-ranked woman in the country. At the highest levels of achievement some men still find humiliation in competing (and potentially coming up short) against women. Why does it hurt more to lose to a girl, unless, deep down, you think girls are worth less than boys? This is an old and deep-seated and in many cases unconscious preju-dice; you can circle the globe and find its gnarly roots wrapped around the foundations of many societies. And just like any other prejudice, cultural or racial, it'll take a long time for it to die out. But shrivel it will, because it's basically a negative, regressive, underground impulse that cannot live in the light of a new day. As we continue to see, societies that look backward and keep their women down fail to keep pace in the modern world. We know for our own 80-year battle to claim our rights that the Founding Fathers weren't thinking of women when they wrote the concept of freedom into our constitution. But you could argue that part of the reason that the West has sustained its ascendancy is due to the exponentially expanding opportunities offered ALL of its citizens.

You, the gentlemen of the graduating class, have expe-rienced life on campus as members of the minority. I hope they didn't give you too hard a time. At least this may have given you an appreciation for the importance of preserving the rights of the few; democracy is devoted to the idea that everyone, not just the majority, deserves a voice. My brothers were taught as boys to open the door for the ladies, a practice they were happy to forget about in the advent of the women's movement. At the leadership level now, however, chivalry of a new sort is called for. I hope when you encounter the success you deserve, and the discrepancy I have talked about, you will respond with speed and grace. The door should be opened for the ladies, the boardroom door, and our gentlemen will have to do it. We all need to be given opportunities, and then we have to disregard all of the statistics that predict we're not likely to reach our goal. Success is often provided by the exception to the Rules for Success. People who have broken through colour and gender lines, class and cultural bias, have done so despite an array of reasons as to why they shouldn't be able to do so. In this way, success may ultimately have more to do with your own personality, focus and optimism than your gender, race or background. Put blinders on to those things that conspire to hold you back, especially the ones in your own head. Guard your good mood. Listen to music every day, joke, and love and read more for fun, especially poetry.

And now I'm going to read you a poem, because I believe that every solemn, joyous, tedious and important rite of passage should and must be celebrated and elevated by poetry. This is 'Begin' by Brendan Kennelly.

Begin again to the summoning birds
to the sight of light at the window,
begin to the roar of morning traffic
all along Pembroke Road.
Every beginning is a promise
born in light and dying in dark
determination and exaltation of springtime
flowering the way to work.
Begin to the pageant of queuing girls
the arrogant loneliness of swans in the canal
bridges linking the past and the future
old friends passing though with us still.
Begin to the loneliness that cannot end
since it perhaps is what makes us begin,
begin to wonder at unknown faces
at crying birds in the sudden rain
at branches stark in the willing sunlight
at seagulls foraging for bread
at couples sharing a sunny secret
alone together while making good.
Though we live in a world that dreams of ending
that always seems about to give in
something that will not acknowledge conclusion
insists that we forever begin.

And lastly, as to the whole sad thing with the Old Man of the Mountain; 200 years ago, Daniel Webster remarked of the rocky crag: 'God has hung out a sign to show that in New England he makes Men.' I say, 'Hmmm … maybe God is changing the sign …'

The mountains may crumble
Gibraltar may crumble
They're only made of clay, But-
Our love is here—to stay!

I speak for all here who send you out into your future with love, respect for your hard work and high happy hopes for each and every one of you. Good luck, and thank you.

SEAMUS HEANEY

GETTING STARTED

University of North Carolina, 1996

C lass of '96, today's date, May 12, will always be a memorable one for you, and for me too. From here on, the mark of the tar is upon all of us, academically and indelibly: so let us rejoice in that, because now we fare forth as Tar Heels of the mind, and the world where we are to make our tarry mark in lies all before us.

But then, when it comes to faring forth, today's date, May 12, has always been an auspicious one. Especially in my native province of Ulster, for long ago it was designated a kind of second May Day, the official start of the summer season; and so May the twelfth became the day when the great hiring fairs took place at towns all over the countryside, when working men and working women would assemble there to be hired out for another term to new masters and mistresses. The hiring fair was a cross between a commencement day and a slave market; it was a carnival shadowed by the tyranny of economic necessity, but it did produce a real sense of occasion. It was a hosting of the local clans and it brought the singer and the musician and the whole community on to the streets, with all their wares and in all their finery; so I thought that I could

13

celebrate this great hosting of the clans here at Chapel Hill and celebrate the old links that have been established between Ulster people who emigrated to North Carolina in the eighteenth century and who played such an important part in the founding of this university – people like the Reverend David Ker, the university's first presiding professor, a graduate of Trinity College, Dublin – I thought I could celebrate that old connection and celebrate, of course, my own new one here today by quoting from a ballad I used to hear when I was growing up in County Derry. It tells the story of a young woman setting out with high hopes of romantic adventure on May the twelfth, to the May Fair at Magherafelt, which is the one sizeable town in our part of the country. But it begins like this:

I am a bouncing fair young girl,
my age is scarce sixteen,
and when I'm dressed all in my best
I look like any queen;
bright, young, at play, who wants a way
to go and sell her wares,
on the twelfth of May I made my way
to Magherafelt May Fair.

My mother's caution unto me
was not stay late in town,

for if you do, my father and I
both on you we will frown.
Be wise and shun bad company
and of young men do beware –
how smart you be, don't make too free
in Magherafelt May Fair.

Well, I would like to quote the whole thing, but at this stage it's enough that the bouncing fair young girl has started on her journey; like the heroine of a thousand other ballads, she has roamed out on a May morning to encounter whatever fortune puts in her way. And over the years, because of her confidence and buoyancy, she has become for me the guardian angel of all such moments of faring forth; for it matters very little on occasions like this whether you are the tomboy daughter of God-fearing rural parents in nineteenth-century Ulster or the atheist heir of tobacco barons in our own date – what matters at these occasions is not the economic givens of your background but the state of readiness of your own spirit. In fact, the ability to start out upon your own impulse is fundamental to the gift of keeping going upon your own terms, not to mention the further and more fulfilling gift of getting again all over again – never resting upon the oars of success or in the doldrums of disappointment, but getting renewed and revived by some further transformation.

Getting started,
keeping going,
getting started again
– in art and in life …
this is the essential
rhythm not only of
achievement but of
survival.

Getting started, keeping going, getting started again –
in art and in life, it seems to me this is the essential rhythm
not only of achievement but of survival, the ground of
convinced action, the basis of self-esteem and the guarantee of credibility in your lives, credibility to yourselves as
well as to others. So this rhythm is what I would like to
talk about briefly this morning, because it is something
I would want each one of you to experience in the years
ahead, and experience not only in your professional life,
whatever that may be, but in your emotional and spiritual
lives as well – because unless that underground level of the
self is preserved as a verified and verifying element in your
make-up, you are going to be in danger of settling into
whatever profile the world prepares for you and accepting
whatever profile the world provides for you. You'll be in
danger of moulding yourselves in accordance with laws
of growth other than those of your own intuitive being.

The world, for example, expects a commencement
speaker to arrive with a set of directives, a complete do-it-
yourself success kit, which he or she then issues to the
graduating class; the commencement speaker's appointed
role is to provide a clear-cut map of the future and a key
to navigating it as elegantly and profitably as possible.
To be a mixture of Polonius and Tiresias, of bore and
of bard. But while that is what the world prescribes, the
inner laws of this particular speaker's being make him
extremely anxious about laying down laws or mapping

17

the future for anybody. In fact, this speaker believes that all those laws and directions have to be personal discoveries rather than prescribed routes; they must be part and parcel of each individual's sense of the world. They are to be improvised rather than copied, they are to be invented rather than imitated, they are to be risked and earned rather than bought into. Indeed, I have to say that for me, this very commencement address has been a matter of risk and improvisation from the moment I said I would do it, because I kept asking myself how I could reconcile my long-standing aversion to the know-all with a desire to say something worthwhile to you.

I therefore did what I increasingly do in moments of crisis nowadays: I asked my daughter what I should do. 'Just be yourself, Dad,' she said. 'Talk about yourself. Tell them a few stories.' And this advice was a great relief to me because I thought, 'Yes, that's true. Some of the greatest wisdom-speakers in the world went about their work that way. So Seamus what was good enough for Aesop and for Jesus should be good enough for you. Relax. For a start, for a start, tell them something about getting started.'

Like for example, the Russian poet and novelist Boris Pasternak's definition of talent. Talent and the art of writing is 'boldness in face of the blank sheet'. The sheer exhilaration of those words is already enough to convince you of their truth, the truth that getting started is more than half the battle. One of the great Sufi teachers expressed the same wisdom in a slightly different way. 'A great idea', he said, 'will come to you three times. If you go with it the first time, it will do nearly all the work for you. Even if you don't move until the second time, it will still do half the work for you. But if you leave it until the third time, you will have to do all the work yourself.'

My own story in this regard, however, is more a story about a false start, although it is indeed a story about the importance of getting started from that first base of your being, the place of ultimate suffering and ultimate decisions in each of you, the last ditch and the first launching pad. When I was in primary school, I was once asked to do a composition entitled 'a day at the seaside' – a common, indeed a predictable subject in a country school in Northern Ireland years ago. So, I wrote about the sunlit sand, of the yachts in the bay, of the perfect sandcastles and of diving in the pool, even though the weather was usually rainy and it was a coal boat rather than a yacht in the bay and I was a farmer's son who couldn't have passed through the University of Carolina because I couldn't in fact swim at all, never mind diving into a pool. But my chief lyrical effort was reserved for the description of the bucket and the spade I said I had used at the beach. The sky-blue enamelled inside of the bucket, as bright as a graduating class at the University of North Carolina, and the technicolour outside, all its little canary yellows and greenfinch greens and canary yellows. And then I also praised the little spade for being so trimly shafted, so youngster-friendly, so small and scaled down. And so I got my grade for making up a fantasy and delivering the conventional goods, pictures I had seen on postcards of other people's days at the seaside. But years later what came back to me was the thing I did not describe, the truth I had suppressed about a day which had actually been a day of bittersweet disappointment. An account of what had actually happened would have been far more convincing as a piece of writing than the conventional account I had rendered up, far truer to life altogether.

I have to say this even if it is on Mother's Day, but when my mother was out for the day – indeed especially when she was out for the day – she was a frugal woman, far too self-denying and far too much in thrall to the idea of keeping going to indulge herself or her children in the luxury of catchpennies that she would see like buckets and spades. After all, we were only out for the day; next morning we'd be back on the land, up in the morning for our porridge, out to the field to bring the cows to the byre and after that to deliver the milk to our neighbours. But still, in her mother's heart, she desperately wanted to do something for us, so off she went to a hardware store and bought not the conventional seaside gear that we desired but a consignment of down-to-earth farm equipment which she could utilize when she went home: instead of bucket and spade, she brought us a plain tin milkcan and a couple of wooden spoons, durable items indeed, useful enough in their own way, but wooden spoons for God's sakes, totally destructive of all glamour and all magic. I hope it will be obvious why I tell you this: I want to avoid preaching at you but I do want to convince you that the true and durable path into and through experience involves being true to the actual givens of your lives. True to your own solitude, true to your own secret knowledge. Because oddly enough, it is that intimate, deeply personal knowledge that links us most vitally and keeps us most reliably connected to one another. Calling a spade a spade may be a bit reductive but calling a wooden spoon a wooden spoon is the beginning of wisdom. And you will be sure to keep going in life on a far steadier keel and with far more radiant individuality if you navigate by that principle.

Luckily, in a commencement address you only have to get started and keep going. Luckily for you and for me there is no necessity to start again. But for you today, Class of 1996, starting again is what it is actually all about. By graduating from this great and famous university, you have reached a stepping stone in your life, a place where you can pause for a moment and enjoy the luxury of looking back on the distance covered; but the thing about stepping stones is that you always need to find another one up there ahead of you. Even if it is panicky

Calling a spade a spade may be a bit reductive but calling a wooden spoon a wooden spoon is the beginning of wisdom.

in midstream, there is no going back. The next move is always the test. Even if the last move did not succeed, the inner command says move again. Even if the hopes you started out with are dashed, hope has to be maintained. Back in Magherafelt May Fair, for example, our young woman didn't dazzle the crowd as thoroughly as she had hoped she would. The song ends like this:

So I bade them all good evening
*   and there I hoisted sail,*
Let the best betide my countryside,
*   my fortune never fail.*
Then night coming on, all hopes being gone,
*   I think I will try elsewhere,*
at a dance or a wake my chance I'll take
*   and leave Magherafelt May Fair.*

Class of 1996, Tar Heels of the mind, when I said at the beginning that the world was all before you, I was echoing what the English poet John Milton said at the end of his great poem, *Paradise Lost*. And I am not the first one to have echoed that line. Almost a century-and-a-half after Milton wrote about Adam and Eve being driven out of Eden, into history, having to keep going by the sweat of their brow, Milton's words were echoed by another English poet, William Wordsworth, at the start of his epoch-making autobiographical poem, *The Prelude*. By making the entry into adult experience an adventure rather than a penalty, Wordsworth was announcing the theme I have addressed this morning; he was implying that history, and our individual lives within history, constantly involve the same effort at starting again and again.

Whether it be a matter of personal relations within a marriage or political initiatives within a peace process, there is no sure-fire do-it-yourself kit. There is risk and truth to yourselves and the world before you. But there is a pride and joy also, a pride and joy that is surging through this crowd today, through the emotions of your parents and your mothers particularly on Mother's Day, your families and your assembled friends. And through you yourselves especially. And so, my fellow graduates, make the world before you a better one by going into it with all boldness. You are up to it and you are fit for it; you deserve it and if you make your own best contribution, the world before you will become a bit more deserving of you.

TONI MORRISON

THE WORLD YOU INHERIT

Wellesley College, 2004

have to confess to all of you, Madame President, Board of Trustees, members of the faculty, relatives, friends, students. I have had some conflicted feelings about accepting this invitation to deliver the commencement address to Wellesley's Class of 2004. My initial response, of course, was glee, a very strong sense of pleasure at, you know, participating personally and formally in the rites of an institution with this reputation: 125 years of history in women's education, an enviable rostrum of graduates, its commitment sustained over the years in making a difference in the world and its successful resistance to challenges that women's colleges have faced from the beginning and throughout the years. An extraordinary record and I was delighted to be asked to participate and return to this campus.

But my second response was not so happy. I was very anxious about having to figure out something to say to this particular class at this particular time, because I was really troubled by what could be honestly said in 2004 to over 500 elegantly educated women, or to relatives and friends who are relieved at this moment, but hopeful as well as apprehensive. And to a college faculty and administration dedicated to leadership and knowledgeable about what that entails. Well, of course, I could be sure of the relatives and the friends, just tell them that youth is always insulting because it manages generation after generation not only to survive and replace us, but to triumph over us completely.

And I would remind the faculty and the administration of what each knows: that the work they do takes second place to nothing, nothing at all, and that theirs is a first-order profession. Now, of course to the graduates I could make reference to things appropriate to your situations – the future, the past, the present, but most of all happiness. Regarding the future, I would have to rest my case on some bromide, like the future is yours for the taking. Or, that it's whatever you make of it. But the fact is it is not yours for the taking. And it is not whatever you make of it. The future is also what other people make of it, how other people will participate in it and impinge on your experience of it.

But I'm not going to talk any more about the future because I'm hesitant to describe or predict because I'm not even certain that it exists. That is to say, I'm not certain that somehow, perhaps, a burgeoning ménage à trois of political interests, corporate interests and military interests will not prevail and literally annihilate an inhabitable, humane future. Because I don't think we

The future is also
what other people
make of it, how other
people will
participate in it and
impinge on your
experience of it.

can any longer rely on separation of powers, free speech, religious tolerance or unchallengeable civil liberties as a matter of course. That is, not while finite humans in the flux of time make decisions of infinite damage. Not while finite humans make infinite claims of virtue and unassailable power that are beyond their competence, if not their reach. So, no happy talk about the future.

Maybe the past offers a better venue. You already share an old tradition of an uncompromisingly intellectual women's college, and that past and that tradition is important to both understand and preserve. It's worthy of reverence and transmission. You've already learned some strategies for appraising the historical and economical and cultural past that you have inherited. But this is not a speech focusing on the splendour of the national past that you are also inheriting.

You will detect a faint note of apology in the descriptions of this bequest, a kind of sorrow that accompanies it, because it's not good enough for you. Because the past is already in debt to the mismanaged present. And besides, contrary to what you may have heard or learned, the past is not done and it is not over, it's still in process, which is another way of saying that when it's critiqued, analysed, it yields new information about itself. The past is already changing as it is being re-examined, as it is being listened to for deeper resonances. Actually it can be more liberating than any imagined future if you are willing to identify its evasions, its distortions, its lies, and are willing to unleash its secrets.

But again, it seemed inappropriate, very inappropriate, for me to delve into a past for people who are in the process of making one, forging their own, so I consider this focusing on your responsibility as graduates – graduates of this institution and citizens of the world – and to tell you once again, repeat to you the admonition, a sort of a wish, that you go out and save the world. That is to suggest to you that with energy and right thinking you can certainly improve, certainly you might even rescue it. Now that's a heavy burden to be placed on one generation by a member of another generation because it's a responsibility we ought to share, not save the world, but simply to love it, meaning don't hurt it, it's already beaten and scoured and gasping for breath. Don't hurt it or enable others who do and will. Know and identify the predators waving flags made of dollar bills. They will say anything, promise anything, do everything to turn the planet into a casino where only the house cards can win – little people with finite lives love to play games with the infinite. But I thought better of that, selecting your responsibilities for you. If I did that, I would assume your education had been in vain and that you were incapable of deciding for yourself what your responsibilities should be.

So, I'm left with the last thing that I sort of ignored as a topic. Happiness. I'm sure you have been told that this is the best time of your life. It may be. But if it's true that this is the best time of your life, if you have already lived or are now living at this age the best years, or if the next few turn out to be the best, then you have my condolences. Because you'll want to remain here, stuck in these so-called best years, never maturing, wanting only to look, to feel and be the adolescent that whole industries are devoted to forcing you to remain.

One more flawless article of clothing, one more elaborate toy, the truly perfect diet, the harmless but necessary drug, the almost final elective surgery, the ultimate cosmetic – all designed to maintain hunger for stasis. While children are being eroticized into adults, adults are being exoticized into eternal juvenilia. I know that happiness has been the real, if covert, target of your labours here, your choices of companions, of the profession that you will enter. You deserve it and I want you to gain it, everybody should. But if that's all you have on your mind, then you do have my sympathy, and if these are indeed the best years of your life, you do have my condolences because there is nothing, believe me, more satisfying, more gratifying than true adulthood. The adulthood that is the span of life before you. The process of becoming one is not inevitable. Its achievement is a difficult beauty, an intensely hard-won glory, which commercial forces and cultural vapidity should not be permitted to deprive you of.

Now, if I can't talk inspiringly and hopefully about the future or the past or the present and your responsibility to the present or happiness, you might be wondering why I showed up. If things are that dour, that tentative, you might ask yourself, what's this got to do with me? What about my life? I didn't ask to be born, as they say. I beg to differ with you. Yes, you did! In fact, you insisted upon it. It's too easy, you know, too ordinary, too common to not be born. So your presence here on earth is a very large part your doing.

So it is up to the self, that self that insisted on life that I want to speak to now – candidly – and tell you the truth that I have not really been clear-headed about, the world I have described to you, the one you are inheriting. All my ruminations about the future, the past, responsibility, happiness are really about my generation, not yours. My generation's profligacy, my generation's heedlessness and denial, its frail ego that required endless draughts of power juice and repeated images of weakness in others in order to prop up our own illusion of strength, more and more self-congratulation while we sell you more and more games and images of death as entertainment. In short, the palm I was reading wasn't yours, it was the splayed hand of my own generation and I know no generation has a complete grip on the imagination and work of the next one, not mine and not your parents', not if you refuse to let it be so. You don't have to accept those media labels. You need not settle for any defining category. You don't have to be merely a taxpayer or a red state or a blue state or a consumer or a minority or a majority.

Of course, you're general, but you're also specific. A citizen and a person, and the person you are is like nobody else on the planet. Nobody has the exact memory that you have. What is now known is not all what you are capable of knowing. You are your own stories and therefore free to imagine and experience what it means to be human without wealth. What it feels like to be human without domination over others, without reckless arrogance, without fear of others unlike you, without rotating, rehearsing and reinventing the hatreds you learned in the sandbox. And although you don't have complete control over the narrative (no author does, I can tell you), you could nevertheless create it.

Although you will never fully know or successfully manipulate the characters who surface or disrupt your plot, you can respect the ones who do by paying them close attention and doing them justice. The theme you choose may change or simply elude you, but being your own story means you can always choose the tone. It also means that you can invent the language to say who you are and what you mean. But then, I am a teller of stories and therefore an optimist, a believer in the ethical bend of the human heart, a believer in the mind's disgust with fraud and its appetite for truth, a believer in the ferocity of beauty. So, from my point of view, which is that of a storyteller, I see your life as already artful, waiting, just waiting and ready for you to make it art.

Thank you.

ARNOLD SCHWARZENEGGER

SIX RULES OF SUCCESS

University of Southern Carolina, 2009

W ell, thank you very much. Hello, everybody. What a great introduction, what a wonderful thing. What a great, great welcome I'm getting here, so thank you very much. I mean, I haven't heard applause like that since I announced that I was going to stop acting.

But anyway, it is really terrific to see here so many graduate students and undergraduate students graduating here today. I heard that there are 4,500 graduating here today, undergraduate students, so this is fantastic. There are 2,200 men, 2,300 women and five have listed yourselves as undecided. So this is really a great, great bunch of people here, I love it.

But seriously, President Sample, trustees, faculty, family, friends and graduates, it is a tremendous privilege to stand before you this morning. There's nothing that I enjoy more than celebrating great achievements. And I don't just mean your parents celebrating never having to pay another tuition bill, that's not what I'm talking about. I'm talking about just celebrating the great accomplishment.

So let me congratulate the Trojan Class of 2009 on your graduation from one of the finest universities in the world. Let's give our graduates a tremendous round of applause. What a special day, what a great accomplishment.

Now, this is an equally special day, of course, for the parents, for the grandparents, siblings and other family members whose support made all of this today possible. And let's not forget, of course, the professors, those dedicated individuals who taught you, who came up with exciting ways to share their vast wisdom, knowledge and experience with you.

And I must also say thank you to President Sample for honouring me with this fantastic degree. Thank you very much. Wow, Arnold Schwarzenegger, Doctor of Humane Letters. I love it.

But, of course, I noticed that it wasn't a doctorate in film or in cinema or in acting. I wonder why? But anyway, that's OK. I take whatever I can get. But maybe now since I'm the doctor, I can go back up to Sacramento and maybe now the legislature will finally listen to me.

But anyway, I stand before you today not just as Dr Schwarzenegger or as Governor Schwarzenegger, or as The Terminator, or as Conan the Barbarian, but also as a proud new member of this Trojan family.

Now, some of you may know that my daughter just completed her freshman year right here. One of the most exciting things for me has been to learn about the great traditions that make this university so wonderful and so special. My daughter told me all about, for instance, the Victory Bell. She sat me down and she told me it weighs 295 pounds and how the winner of the annual football game between USC and UCLA takes this bell and gets to paint it in the school colours. And I stopped her in the middle of talking, I said, 'Wait a minute, Katherine, back up a little bit. UCLA has a football team?'

Now, of course, my daughter's journey here at USC is just beginning, and yours is ending. I know that you're a little bit stressed out right now as you start this exciting new chapter in your lives. Some people say it is scary to leave the comfort of the university and to go out into the cold, hard world. But I have to tell you something; I think this is a bunch of nonsense because after all, this is America. This is the greatest country on earth, with the greatest opportunities.

It is one thing if you were born in Afghanistan or in Swat Valley in Pakistan where you'd be forced to join the Taliban or be killed. Now, then I would say yes, that is a little bit scary. But this, this is going to be a piece of cake for you, trust me. You live in America and you're prepared for the future with this tremendous education you have gotten here at one of the greatest universities in the world. This is going to be exciting, it's a great adventure and this is a new phase in your life. This is going to be awesome.

Now, of course, this journey is not going to be without any setbacks, failures or disappointments. That's just the way life is. But you're ready and you are able, and you would not be here today with your degrees and with your honours if you wouldn't be ready.

So now, of course, to help you along the way, I thought that the best Schwarzenegger gift I could give you today is to give you a few of my own personal ideas on how to be successful. And parents, I just want you to know, maybe you should close your ears, you should plug your ears, because maybe there a few things that you maybe won't like in what I have to say. But anyway, I can explain how I became successful and who I am today by going through what I call Dr Schwarzenegger's Six Rules of Success.

Now, of course, people ask me all the time, they say to me, 'What is the secret to success?' And I give them always the short version. I say, 'Number one, come to America. Number two, work your butt off. And number three, marry a Kennedy.' But anyway, those are the short rules.

Now today, I'm going to give you the six rules of success. But before I start, I just wanted to say these are my rules. I think that they can apply to anyone, but that is for you to decide, because not everyone is the same. There are some people that just like to kick back and coast through life and others want to be very intense and want to be number one and want to be successful.

And that's like me. I always wanted to be very intense, I always wanted to be number one. I took it very seriously, my career. So this was the same when I started

with bodybuilding. I didn't want to just be a bodybuilding champion, I wanted to be the best bodybuilder of all
time. The same was in the movies. I didn't want to just be
a movie star; I wanted to be a great movie star that is the
highest-paid movie star and have above-the-title billing.
And so this intensity always paid off for me, this commitment always paid off for me.

So here are some of the rules. The first rule is: trust
yourself.

And what I mean by that is, so many young people
are getting so much advice from their parents and from
their teachers and from everyone. But what is most
important is that you have to dig deep down, dig deep
down and ask yourselves, who do you want to be?
Not what, but who. And I'm talking about not what
your parents and teachers want you to be, but you. I'm
talking about figuring out for yourselves what makes
you happy, no matter how crazy it may sound to other
people.

I was lucky growing up because I did not have
television or didn't have telephones, I didn't have the
computers and the iPods. And, of course, Twitter was
then something that birds did outside the window. I
didn't have all these distractions and all this. I spent a
lot of time by myself, so I could figure out and listen to
what is inside my heart and inside my head. And I recog-
nized very quickly that inside my head and heart were

a burning desire to leave my small village in Austria – not that there was something wrong with Austria, it's a beautiful country. But I wanted to leave that little place and I wanted to be part of something big, the United States of America, a powerful nation, the place where dreams can come true. I knew when I came over here I could realize my dreams.

And I decided that the best way for me to come to America was to become a bodybuilding champion, because I knew that was my ticket the instant that I saw a magazine cover of my idol, Reg Park. He was Mr Universe, he was starring in Hercules movies, he looked strong and power-ful, he was so confident. So when I found out how he got that way I became obsessed, and I went home and I said to my family, 'I want to be a bodybuilding champion.'

Now, you can imagine how that went over in my home in Austria. My parents, they couldn't believe it. They would have been just happy if I would have become a police officer like my father, or married someone like Heidi, had a bunch of kids and ran around like the von Trapp family in *The Sound of Music*. That's what my family had in mind for me, but something else burned inside me. Something burned inside me. I wanted to be different; I was determined to be unique. I was driven to think big and to dream big.

Everyone else thought that I was crazy. My friends said, 'If you want to be a champion in a sport, why don't you

Something burned inside me. I wanted to be different; I was determined to be unique. I was driven to think big and to dream big.

go and become a bicycle champion or a skiing champion or a soccer champion? Those are the Austrian sports.' But I didn't care. I wanted to be a bodybuilding champion and use that to come to America, and use that to go into the movies and make millions of dollars.

So, of course, for extra motivation I read books on strongmen and on bodybuilding and looked at magazines. And one of the things I did was, I decorated my bedroom wall. Right next to my bed there was this big wall that I decorated all with pictures. I hung up pictures of strong-men and bodybuilders and wrestlers and boxers and so on.

And I was so excited about this great decoration that I took my mother to the bedroom and I showed her. And she shook her head. She was absolutely in shock and tears started running down her eyes. And she called the doctor, she called our house doctor and she brought him in and she explained to him, 'There's something wrong here.' She looked at the wall with the doctor and she said, 'Where did I go wrong? I mean, all of Arnold's friends have pictures on the wall of girls, and Arnold has all these men. But it's not just men, they're half-naked and they're oiled up with baby oil. What is going on here? Where did I go wrong?'

So you can imagine, the doctor shook his head and he said, 'There's nothing wrong. At this age you have idols and you go and have those – this is just quite normal.'

So this is rule number one. I wanted to become a champion; I was on a mission. So rule number one is, of course, trust yourself, no matter how and what anyone else thinks.

Rule number two is: break the rules. We have so many rules in life about everything. I say break the rules. Not the law, but break the rules. My wife has a T-shirt that says, 'Well-behaved women rarely make history.' Well, you know, I don't want to burst her bubble, but the same is true with men. It is impossible to be a maverick or a true original if you're too well behaved and don't want to break the rules. You have to think outside the box. That's what I believe. After all, what is the point of being on this earth if all you want to do is be liked by everyone and avoid trouble?

The only way that I ever got any place was by breaking some of the rules. After all, I remember that after I was finished with my bodybuilding career I wanted to get into acting and I wanted to be a star in films. You can imagine what the agents said when I went to meet all those agents. Everyone had the same line, that it can't be done, the rules are different here. They said, 'Look at your body. You have this huge monstrous body, overly developed. That doesn't fit into the movies. You don't understand. This was 20 years ago, the Hercules movies. Now the little guys are in, Dustin Hoffman, Woody Allen, Jack Nicholson.' Before he gained weight, of course, that is. But anyway, those are the guys that were in.

And the agents also complained about my accent. They said, 'No one ever became a star with an accent like that, especially not with a German accent. And yes, I can imagine with your name, Arnold Schwartzenschnitzel, or whatever the name is, on a billboard. Yeah, that's going to draw a lot of tickets and sell a lot of tickets. Yeah, right.'

So this is the kind of negative attitude they had.

But I didn't listen to those rules, even though they were very nice and they said, 'Look, we can get you some bit parts. We can get you to be playing a wrestler or a bouncer. Oh, maybe with your German accent we can get you to be a Nazi officer in *Hogan's Heroes* or something like that.'

But I didn't listen to all this. Those were their rules, not my rules. I was convinced I could do it if I worked as hard as I did in bodybuilding, five hours a day. And I started getting to work, I started taking acting classes. I took English classes, took speech classes, dialogue classes. Accent removal classes I even took. I remember running around saying, 'A fine wine grows on the vine.' You see, because Germans have difficulties with the F and the W and V, so, 'A fine wine grows on the vine.' I know what some of you are now saying, is I hope that Arnold got his money back. But let me tell you something, I had a good time doing those things and it really helped me.

And finally I broke through. I broke through and I started getting the first parts in TV; *Streets of San Francisco*, Lucille Ball hired me, I made *Pumping Iron*,

Stay Hungry. And then I got the big break in *Conan the Barbarian*. And there the director said, 'If we wouldn't have Schwarzenegger we would have to build one.' Now, think about that. And then, when I did *Terminator*, 'I'll be back' became one of the most famous lines in movie history, all because of my crazy accent. Now, think about it. The things that the agents said would be totally a detriment and would make it impossible for me to get a job, all of a sudden became an asset for me, all of those things, my accent, my body and everything. So it just shows to you, never listen to that you can't do something.

And, 'You have to work your way up, of course, run for something else first.' I mean, it was the same when I ran for governor, the same lines, that you have to work your way up, it can't be done. And then, of course, I ran for governor and the rest, of course, is history. They said you have to start with a small job as mayor and then as assemblyman and then as lieutenant governor and then as governor. And they said that's the way it works in a political career.

I said, 'I'm not interested in a political career. I want to be a public servant. I want to fix California's problems and bring people together and bring the parties together.' So, like I said, I decided to run, I didn't pay attention to the rules. And I made it and the rest is history.

Which, of course, brings me to rule number three: don't be afraid to fail.

Anything I've ever attempted, I was always willing to fail. In the movie business, I remember, that you pick scripts. Many times you think this is a winning script, but then, of course, you find out later on, when you do the movie, that it didn't work and the movie goes in the toilet. Now, we have seen my movies; I mean, *Red Sonja*, *Hercules in New York*, *Last Action Hero*. Those movies went in the toilet. But that's OK, because at the same time I made movies like *Terminator* and *Conan* and *True Lies* and *Predator* and *Twins* that went through the roof.

So you can't always win, but don't be afraid of making decisions. You can't be paralysed by fear of failure or you will never push yourself. You keep pushing because you believe in yourself and in your vision and you know that it is the right thing to do, and success will come. So don't be afraid to fail.

Which brings me to rule number four, which is: don't listen to the naysayers.

How many times have you heard that you can't do this and you can't do that and it's never been done before? Just imagine if Bill Gates had quit when people said it can't be done.

I hear this all the time. As a matter of fact, I love it when someone says that no one has ever done this before, because then when I do it that means that I'm the first one that has done it. So pay no attention to the people that say it can't be done.

I remember my mother-in-law, Eunice Kennedy Shriver, when she started the Special Olympics in 1968, people said that it would not work. The experts, the doctors that specialized in mental disabilities and mental retardation said, 'It can't be done. You can't bring people out of their institutions. You can't make them participate in sports, in jumping and swimming and in running. They will hurt themselves, they will hurt each other, they will drown in the pool.'

Well, let me tell you something. Now, 40 years later, Special Olympics is one of the greatest organizations, in 164 countries, dedicated to people with mental disabilities and that are intellectually challenged. And she did not take no for an answer.

And the same is when you look at Barack Obama. I mean, imagine, if he would have listened. If he would have listened to the naysayers he would have never run for president. People said it couldn't be done, that he couldn't get elected, that he couldn't beat Hillary Clinton, that he would never win the general election. But he followed his own heart, he didn't listen to the 'You can't' and he changed the course of American history.

So over and over you see that. If I would have listened to the naysayers I would still be in the Austrian Alps yodelling. I would never have come to America. I would have never met my wonderful wife Maria Shriver, I would have never had the wonderful four kids, I would have never done *Terminator*, and I wouldn't be standing here in front of you today as governor of the greatest state of the greatest country in the world. So I never listen to that, 'You can't'. I always listen to myself and say, 'Yes, you can'.

And that brings me to rule number five, which is the most important rule of all: work your butt off.

You never want to fail because you didn't work hard enough. I never wanted to lose a competition or lose an election because I didn't work hard enough. I always believed in leaving no stone unturned. Muhammad Ali, one of my great heroes, had a great line in the seventies when he was asked, 'How many sit-ups do you do?'

He said, 'I don't count my sit-ups. I only start counting when it starts hurting. When I feel pain, that's when I start counting, because that's when it really counts.' That's what makes you a champion.

And that's the way it is with everything. No pain, no gain. So many of those lessons that I apply in life I have learned from sports, let me tell you, and especially that one. And let me tell you, it is important to have fun in life, of course. But when you're out there partying, horsing around, someone out there at the same time is working hard. Someone is getting smarter and someone is winning. Just remember that.

Now, if you want to coast through life, don't pay attention to any of those rules. But if you want to win, there is absolutely no way around hard, hard work. None of my rules, by the way, of success, will work unless you do.

I've always figured out that there are 24 hours a day. You sleep 6 hours and have 18 hours left. Now, I know there are some of you out there that say well, wait a minute, I sleep 8 hours or 9 hours. Well, then, just sleep faster, I would recommend. Because you only need to sleep 6 hours and then you have 18 hours left, and there are a lot of things you can accomplish. As a matter of fact, Ed Turner used to say always, 'Early to bed, early to rise, work like hell and advertise.'

And, of course, all of you know already those things, because otherwise you wouldn't be sitting here today. Just remember, you can't climb the ladder of success with your hands in your pockets.

And that takes me to rule number six, which is a very important rule: it's about giving back.

Whatever path that you take in your lives, you must always find time to give something back, something back to your community, give something back to your state or to your country. My father-in-law, Sargent Shriver – who is a great American, a truly great American who started the Peace Corps, the Job Corps, Legal Aid to the Poor – he said at Yale University to the students at a commencement speech, 'Tear down that mirror. Tear down that mirror

If you want to win, there is absolutely no way around hard, hard work. None of my rules, by the way, of success, will work unless you do.

that makes you always look at yourself, and you will be able to look beyond that mirror and you will see the millions of people that need your help.'

And let me tell you something, reaching out and helping people will bring you more satisfaction than anything else you have ever done. As a matter of fact today, after having worked for Special Olympics and having started after-school programs, I've promoted fitness, and now with my job as governor, I can tell you, playing a game of chess with an eight-year-old kid in an inner-city school is far more exciting for me than walking down another red carpet or a movie premiere.

So let me tell you, as you prepare to go off into the world, remember those six rules:

Trust yourself,
Break some rules,
Don't be afraid to fail,
Ignore the naysayers,
Work like hell, and
Give something back.

And now let me leave you with one final thought, and I will be brief, I promise. This university was conceived in 1880, back when Los Angeles was just a small frontier town. One hundred and twenty-five classes of Trojans have gone before you. They have sat there, exactly where you sit today, in good times and in bad, in times of war and in times of peace, in times of great promise and in times of great uncertainty. Through it all, this great country, this great state, this great university, have stood tall and persevered. We are in tough times now and there's a lot of uncertainty in the world.

But there is one thing certain; we'll be back. And we will back stronger and more prosperous than ever before, because that is what California and America have always done. The ancient Trojans were known for their fighting spirit, their refusal to give up, their ability to overcome great odds. So as you graduate today, never lose that optimism and that fighting spirit. Never lose the spirit of Troy. Because remember, this is America and you are USC Trojans, proud, strong and ready to soar.

Congratulations and God bless all of you. Thank you very much. Thank you.

LIN-MANUEL MIRANDA

THE STORY YOU TELL

University of Pennsylvania, 2016

Thank you President Gutmann, MC Provost, Board of Trustees, faculty, family, Mister Vice President, undergrads of the four Penn Schools of Hufflepuff, Slytherin, Ravenclaw and Gryffindor, and dear exhausted, exhilarated, terrified graduates of the Class of 2016.

I begin with an apology.

I am the writer of *Hamilton: An American Musical*. Every word in the show – and there are over 22,000 words in the show – were chosen and put in a really specific order by me. So I am painfully aware that neither Philly nor the great state of Pennsylvania is mentioned in *Hamilton*, with the exception of *one* couplet in the song 'Hurricane', where Hamilton sings:

I wrote my way out of Hell
I wrote my way to Revolution,
I was louder than the crack in The Bell.

That's it! One blink and you miss it, the Liberty Bell reference!

I am also painfully aware that this commencement address is being livestreamed and disseminated all over the world instantly. In fact, 'painfully aware' is pretty much my default state. 'Oh yeah, that's Lin, he's … *painfully* aware.'

So, with the eyes of the world and history on us all, I'd like to correct the record and point out that a few parts in *Hamilton: An American Musical* actually took place in Pennsylvania.

The Battle of Monmouth, wherein General Charles Lee, in our show, 'S'ed the bed' and retreated against Washington's orders. According to Lafayette, this was the only time he ever heard George Washington curse out loud. That's right, the father of our country dropped his choicest profanity and F-bombs in Pennsylvania.

The Constitutional Convention, wherein Alexander Hamilton spoke extemporaneously for six hours in what is surely the most un-tweet-able freestyle of all time, happened right here in Philly.

In fact, Alexander Hamilton lived at 79 South 3rd Street when he began his extramarital affair with Maria Reynolds, creating the time-honoured precedent of political sex scandals and mea culpa. You guys, *The Good Wife* wouldn't even *exist* if Hamilton hadn't gotten the ball rolling on this dubious American tradition, right on South 3rd street, right near the Così.

Finally, I need to apologize on behalf of the historical Alexander Hamilton, because if he hadn't sat down to dinner with James Madison and Thomas Jefferson, desperate for support for his financial plan, Philadelphia might well still be the US Capitol.

Hamilton traded Philly away in the most significant backroom deal in American history. As the guy who plays Hamilton every night, let me get into character for a moment and say, 'My bad, Philadelphia.' Thank you.

But take the long view, Motown Philly. Who really won that deal in the end? Look at DC: it's synonymous with institutional dysfunction, partisan infighting and political gridlock. *You* are known as the birthplace of Louisa May Alcott, Rocky Balboa, Boyz II Men, Betsy Ross, Will Smith, Isaac Asimov, Tina Fey, cheesesteaks, and you can have *scrapple, soft pretzels and Wawa hoagies whenever you want.*

You win, Philly. You win every time. Water ice.

The simple truth is this: every story you choose to tell, by necessity, omits others from the larger narrative. One could write five totally different musicals from Hamilton's eventful, singular American life, without ever overlapping incidents. For every detail I chose to dramatize, there are ten I left out. I include King George at the expense of Ben Franklin. I dramatize Angelica Schuyler's intelligence and heart at the expense of Benedict Arnold's betrayal. James Madison and Hamilton were friends and political allies, but their personal and political fall-out occurs right on our act break, during intermission. My goal is to give you as much as an evening of musical entertainment can provide, and have you on your way home slightly before *Les Mis* lets out next door.

This act of choosing – the stories we tell versus the stories we leave out – will reverberate across the rest of your life. Don't believe me? Think about how you celebrated this Senior Week, and contrast that with the version you shared with the parents and grandparents sitting behind you.

Penn, don't front. You're a *Playboy* magazine ranked party school – you *know* you did things this week that you're never mentioning again. I know what you did this summer!

I'm going to tell you a story from my twenties today – a story I've never told in public before. I'll tell you two stories actually. It's my hope that it'll be of use to you as you stare down the quarter-life marker.

I am 20 years old, finishing my sophomore year at Wesleyan, and my girlfriend of four and a half years is home from her semester abroad. I cannot wait to see her again – she is my first love. I dread seeing her again – I've grown into my life without her. In her absence, with time and angst to spare, I have developed the first draft of my first full-length musical, an 80-minute one-act called *In the Heights*. I have also developed a blinding pain in my right shoulder, which I can't seem to stop cracking. My girlfriend comes home. I am so happy to see her, even as my shoulder

This act of choosing – the stories we tell versus the stories we leave out – will reverberate across the rest of your life.

worsens. My mother takes me to a back specialist, ranked in *New York* magazine, so you know he's good.

He examines me, looks me dead in the eyes, and says, 'There's nothing wrong with your back. There will be if you keep cracking it, but what you have is a nervous tic. Is there anything in your life that is causing you stress?' I burst into tears, in his office. He looks at me for a long time, as I'm crying, and get this – you'll appreciate this, Renée – he tells me the story of Giuseppe Verdi. A nineteenth-century Italian composer of some note, who, in the space of a few short years, lost his wife and two young children to disease. He tells me that Verdi's greatest works – *Rigoletto, La Traviata* – came not before, but after this season of Job, the darkest moments of his life. He looks me in the eyes and tells me, 'You're trying to avoid going through pain, or causing pain. I'm here to tell you that you'll have to survive it if you want to be any kind of artist.'

I break up with my girlfriend that night.

I spend the summer in therapy. I tell a lot of stories I've never told before.

My father asks my mother, 'What the hell kind of back doctor … Verdi? Really?'

I stop cracking my shoulder.

The story I had been telling myself – happy guy in a long-distance relationship with his high-school sweet-heart – was being physically rejected by my body via my shoulder. I'd never broken up with anyone before – in my head, I was a 'good guy', and 'good guys' don't break up with their significant others when one of them goes off to study abroad. I was trying to fit my life into a romantic narrative that was increasingly at odds with how I really felt. In retrospect, we both were.

What about her story? Well, it's not mine to tell, but I can share this much: she began dating one of her good friends the following year of college. Fast-forward to present day: she is happily married to that same good friend, with two beautiful kids. In her story, I am not the angsty, shoulder-cracking tortured artist. I'm the obstacle in the way of the real love story. For you *Office* fans: they're Jim and Pam, and I'm Roy.

Story number two: I am out of college, I am 23 years old, and Tommy Kail and I are meeting with a veteran theatre producer. To pay rent I am a professional substitute teacher: at my old high school. Tommy is Audra McDonald's assistant. Tommy is directing *In the Heights*, and with his genius brain in my corner, my 80-minute one-act is now two acts. This big-deal theatre producer has seen a reading we put on in the basement of the Drama Book Shop in mid-Manhattan, and he is giving us his thoughts. We hang on his every word, this is a big-deal theatre producer, and we are kids, desperate to get our show on. We are discussing the character of Nina Rosario, home from her first year at Stanford, the first in her family to go to college.

The big-deal theatre producer says:

'Now I know in your version Nina's coming home with a secret from her parents: she's lost her scholarship. The song is great, the actress is great. What I'm bumping up against, fellas, is that this doesn't feel high *stakes* enough. Scholarship? Big deal. What if she's pregnant? What if her boyfriend at school hit her? What if she got caught with drugs? It doesn't have to be any of those things, you're the writer – but do you see what I'm getting at guys, a way to ramp up the stakes of your story?'

I resist the urge to crack my shoulder.

We get through the meeting and Tommy and I, again alone, look at each other. He knows what I'm going to say before I say it.

'Pregnant—'

'I know.'

'Nina on drugs—'

'I was there.'

'But he wants to put our show up.'

Tommy looks at me. 'That's not the story you want to tell and that's not the show I want to direct. There are ways to raise the stakes that are not *that*. We'll just keep working.'

If I could get in a time machine and watch any point in my life, it would be this moment. The moment where Tommy Kail looked at uncertain, frazzled me, desperate for a production and a life in this business, tempted, and said no for us. I keep subbing, he continues working for Audra, we keep working on *In the Heights* for five years until we find the right producers in Jill Furman and Kevin McCollum and Jeffrey Seller. Until Philly native Quiara Hudes becomes my co-writer and reframes our show around a community instead of a love triangle. Until Alex Lacamoire and Bill Sherman take my songs and made them come to life through their orchestrations. It will be another five years before *Heights* reaches Broadway, exactly as we intended it.

And then the good part: Nina's story that we fought to tell, keeps coming back around in my life. It comes around in letters, or in the countless young men and women who find me on the subway or on college campuses and take my hand and say, 'You don't understand. I was the first in my family to go to college, when I felt out of place like I was drowning I listened to "Breathe", Nina's song, and it got me through.' And I think to myself as these strangers tell me their Nina stories, 'I do understand. And that sounds pretty high stakes to me.'

I know that many of you made miracles happen to get to this day. I know that parents and grandparents and aunts and uncles and family behind you made miracles happen to be here. I know because my family made miracles happen for me to be standing here talking to you, telling stories.

Your stories are essential. Don't believe me?

In a year when politicians traffic in anti-immigrant rhetoric, there is also a Broadway musical reminding us that a broke, orphan immigrant from the West Indies built our financial system. A story that reminds us that since the beginning of the great unfinished symphony that is our American experiment, time and time again, immigrants get the job done.

My dear, terrified graduates – you are about to enter the most uncertain and thrilling period of your lives.

The stories you are about to live are the ones you will be telling your children and grandchildren and therapists.

They are the temp gigs and internships before you find your passion.

They are the cities you live in before the opportunity of a lifetime pops up halfway across the world.

They are the relationships in which you hang on for dear life even as your shoulder cracks in protest.

They are the times you say no to the good opportunities so you can say yes to the best opportunities.

They are what Verdi survived to bring us *La Traviata*.

They are the stories in which you figure out who you are.

There will be moments you remember and whole years you forget.

There will be times when you are Roy and times when you are Jim and Pam.

The stories you are
about to live are the
ones you will be
telling your children
and grandchildren
and therapists.

There will be blind alleys and one-night wonders and soul-crushing jobs and wake-up calls and crises of confidence and moments of transcendence when you are walking down the street and someone will thank you for telling your story because it resonated with their own.

I feel so honoured to be a detail, a minor character in the story of your graduation day.

I feel so honoured to bear witness to the beginning of your next chapter.

I'm painfully aware of what's at stake.

I can't wait to see how it turns out.

Thank you and congratulations to the Class of 2016.

MICHELLE OBAMA

ON EDUCATION

Dillard University, 2014

MRS OBAMA: Oh, my goodness! Good morning!

AUDIENCE: Good morning.

MRS OBAMA: I am so happy to be here with you all. I'm proud to be here in the Big Easy. Look at you all! You look good.

STUDENT: You do too!

MRS OBAMA: Thank you. I want to start by thanking Nicole for that very kind introduction and for sharing her story, which is not too unfamiliar to me – because they told me I couldn't be where I am, too. So I want to thank Nicole. I'm proud of her. Thank you for the selfie; I think that's the first selfie I've done at a commencement. So, Nicole, you're my first.

And of course, I want to thank the Dillard University Choir. Oh, oh, oh! Oh! That's all I can say. It's like you want to start something up in here, right? It's like, now we got a commencement going on up in here. That was beautiful, beautiful. Thank you so much.

I also want to recognize Senator Mary Landrieu, who is here. Let's give her a hand. She has been a strong supporter of this university.

I want to thank the Dillard University Board of Trustees. I want to thank the faculty, the staff and, of course, your tremendous president, Dr Walter Kimbrough. Now, my husband has been called a few things over the years, but he has never had the honour of being referred to as the 'Hip Hop President'.

I also want to thank all the folks from the University of New Orleans for hosting us here today. And I know they're hosting the folks at Southern University at New Orleans for their commencement later on today as well, so we wish them a wonderful day. And thank you for having us.

And of course, I've got to give a big shout-out to all the family members in the crowd, all of the family members – especially to the mothers, because it is the day before Mother's Day. To all the mothers, Happy Mother's Day.

Now, graduates, you all handled your business, right? Just because you were graduating didn't mean you – come on, now. OK, well, if you didn't, you have my permission to get up and go right now, because there is nothing more important – no, no, don't get up. Your mothers would kill you if you got up at this moment. So just stay in your seats, and when this is all over make sure you take care of mom.

But in all seriousness, to all the moms out there – as well as the dads and the grandparents, the uncles, the aunts, the brothers, the sisters, all of you who have helped raise these graduates – you have seen them through their ups and downs, and you have poured your hearts and souls into these men and women. So today is your day, too, and you should be very proud. You really should.

And finally, most of all, I want to congratulate the beautiful and handsome men and women of the Dillard University Class of 2014. Yay! You all have come so far, I know, to make it to this day – from all those early days when the girls were sneaking out of Williams Hall to go see the boys over at the Duals – oh yeah, I did my research – to all those tests you crammed for, to the plans you're making now for your careers, to go on to graduate school.

You all have seen so much. You've witnessed this school's rebirth after the devastation of Hurricane Katrina – the new buildings that replaced the ones you lost, the classrooms that started filling back up again, the service projects that you all have done to help this community bounce back. And I know along the way that each of you has written your own story of resilience and determination to make it here to this day.

For example, as you heard, Nicole was told back in high school that she just wasn't college material. But now she is your class president, and she's headed off to Yale for her graduate degree. So there. That's it.

And I know that some of you may come from tough neighbourhoods; some of you may have lost your homes during Katrina. Maybe you're like DeShawn Dabney, a graduate who was raised by his grandmother – maybe – that's your grandmother, isn't it, DeShawn? Raised by his grandmother while some of his family members were dealing with issues. Maybe just like him, you've been working part-time jobs since you were a teenager to make your dream of going to college come true. And now, today, you're all here ready to walk across this stage and get that diploma.

And no matter what path you took to get here, you all kept your hearts set on this day. You fought through every challenge you encountered, and you earned that degree from this fine university. And in doing so, you are following in the footsteps of all those who came before you, and you have become an indelible part of the history of this school – a history that, as you all know, stretches back to well before the Civil War, back to 1826, the year a child named Emperor Williams was born.

Now, Emperor was born into slavery. But as he grew up, he managed to teach himself to read and write well enough to create a pass that allowed him to come and go around the city without getting hassled. But one day, his master saw the pass and he said, where did you learn to write like that? Now, just imagine the fear Emperor must have felt when he heard that question – because remember, back then it was illegal for a slave to learn to read or write. So who knows what kind of punishment he may have gotten – a beating, a whipping, even worse.

We don't exactly know what happened on that day, but we do know that when Emperor turned 32, after more than three decades in bondage, he became a free man. He decided to stay in New Orleans, and he went on to become a minister – even founded a church right here in town. And in 1869, when abolitionists, missionaries, black folks and white folks came together to create a school for freed slaves here in New Orleans, Emperor was one of the original signers of the charter.

They decided to name the school New Orleans University, because even though most of the classes would be taught at a high-school level or below, oh, their aspirations were much higher than that. And when they laid the cornerstone for that university's first building down on St Charles Avenue, Emperor got a chance to speak.

He said – and these are his words – he said, 'For twenty years I was a slave on these streets. It was a penitentiary offence to educate a Negro. I have seen my fellow-servants whipped for trying to learn; but today here I am [am I], speaking where a building is to be erected for the education of the children of my people.' He goes on to say, 'I wonder if this is the world I was born in.'

See, in the course of his short lifetime, Emperor saw education go from being a crime for black folks to being a real possibility for his kids and grandkids. So no wonder he was asking whether this was the same world he'd been born into. See, for a man like Emperor, getting an education could open up a whole new world of opportunity. An education meant having real power. It meant you could manage your own money. It meant you couldn't get swindled out of land or possessions when somebody told you to just sign on the dotted line; sometimes even determined whether or not you could vote.

So most folks back then saw education as the key to real and lasting freedom. That's why, when New Orleans University and the other African American college in town, Straight University, first opened their doors, one of the biggest problems they faced was too many students. That's right – too many students. Many of these students barely spoke English; they'd grown up speaking Creole or French. Few had ever seen the inside of a classroom or even been taught their ABCs.

But let me tell you, those students were hungry – you hear me? Hungry. They studied like their lives depended on it. They blazed through their lessons. And that hunger for education lasted for generations in the African American community here in New Orleans.

When an arsonist set fire to the school's library in 1877, they built a new one. When those two original schools ran into financial troubles years later, they started making plans to build an even bigger and better university. And in the 1930s, when white folks complained that this new school would mean too many black students on their buses, the folks at the school got the city to add a bus line just for their students, because nothing – nothing – was going to stop them from achieving the vision of those early founders.

And finally, in May of 1934, they broke ground for this school, Dillard University – a university that would go on to produce some of the leading thinkers and achievers in our country. And the day the cornerstone was laid for your library, the president of Howard University spoke these words: He said, 'There lies in this Southland today, buried in unmarked graves, many a black genius who would have blessed this city and this section of our country, if [only] his parents could have had before them the Dillard University you are now building.'

And in the years since then, through segregation and depression, through threats of violence and the floodwaters of a devastating storm, students like you have come here to study and to learn, and to carry forward those hopes and dreams. And today, I stand before a sea of young geniuses. Oh, yeah.

So, graduates, I hope that you understand that this day is not just the culmination of your own dreams, but the realization of the dreams of so many who came before you.

This day is not just the culmination of your own dreams, but the realization of the dreams of so many who came before you.

And you should be so proud, and so happy, and so excited about your futures. But what you shouldn't be is satisfied. See, because while it is a wonderful thing that all of you are here today, we have to ask ourselves, what about all those geniuses who never get this chance?

I'm talking about the young people from right here in New Orleans and across the country who aren't part of a commencement like this one today, kids no different from all of us, kids who never made it out of high school. The fact is that today, the high-school graduation rate for black students is improving, but it is still lower than just about any other group in this country. And while college graduation rates have risen for nearly every other demographic, including African American women, the college graduation rate for African American men has flatlined.

See, and the thing is, when our young people fall behind like that in school, they fall behind in life. Last year, African Americans were more than twice as likely as whites to be unemployed. They were almost three times as likely to live in poverty. And they were far more likely to end up in prison or be the victims of violent crimes.

Now, perhaps when you hear these statistics, you might think to yourself, well, those numbers are terrible, but I'm not part of the problem. And you might be thinking that since you're not one of those statistics, and you're sitting here wearing that nice black robe today, you can go on your way and never look back.

But folks like you and me, we can't afford to think like that – never. See, because we're the lucky ones, and we can never forget that we didn't get where we are today all on our own. We got here today because of so many people who toiled and sweat and bled and died for us – people like our parents and grandparents and all those who came before them, people who never dreamed of getting a college education themselves but who worked, and saved, and sacrificed so that we could be here today. We owe them. We owe them.

And the only way to pay back that debt is by making those same kinds of sacrifices and investments for the next generation. And I know sitting here right now, that task could seem a bit overwhelming. I know it could seem like the deck is stacked way too high against our young people. And the truth is that some of the problems we face – structural inequality, schools that lag behind, workplace and housing discrimination – those problems are too big for one person to fix on their own.

But that's still no excuse to stand on the sidelines. Because we know that today, education is still the key to real and lasting freedom – it is still true today. So it is now up to us to cultivate that hunger for education in our own lives and in those around us. And we know that hunger is still out there – we know it.

We see it in students like DeShawn and Nicole and all of you who scraped and clawed so you could make it to this day. We see it in the single moms who work three jobs so their kids might have a shot at earning a degree like yours. We see that hunger all around the world – in that young woman named Malala who was shot on her school bus in Pakistan just for speaking out in support of girls getting an education, and the more than 200 girls kidnapped from their own school in Nigeria for wanting an education – young people who are knowingly risking their lives every day just to go to school.

And in fact, you've seen that hunger right here at Dillard: your valedictorian, three salutatorians are all from Nigeria. They studied hard at an early age, earned scholarships to come here to this university, achieved 4.0 GPAs. And now they are off pursuing master's degrees, work in software development, teaching math and science to young people here in the United States.

See, now, that's the kind of hunger for education that we have to reignite in all of our communities. It's the same hunger that gave life to this university, the same hunger that defined so many of our parents and grandparents – including my own. You see, my parents never went to college, but they were determined to see me and my brother and all the kids in our neighbourhood get a good education.

So my mother volunteered at my school – helping out every day in the front office, making sure our teachers were doing their jobs, holding their feet to the fire if she thought they were falling short. I'd walk by the office and there she'd be. I'd leave class to go to the bathroom, there she'd be again, roaming the halls, looking in the classrooms. And of course, as a kid, I have to say, that was a bit mortifying, having your mother at school all the time.

But looking back, I have no doubt that my classmates and I got a better education because she was looking over those teachers' shoulders. You see, my mom was not a teacher or a principal or a school-board member. But when it came to education, she had that hunger. So she believed that our education was very much her business.

And we need more people who think and act like my mother, and all those mothers out there, because the education of our young people is all of our business. That's what Emperor Williams thought. That's what the folks here in New Orleans thought as they worked to rebuild this campus after Katrina. And as graduates of Dillard University, that's how we need you to think every single day for the rest of your lives.

You all have opportunities and skills and education that so many folks who came before you never could have dreamed of. So just imagine the kind of impact that you're going to make. Imagine how you can inspire those around you to reach higher and complete their own education.

And you can start small. Start by volunteering at an after-school programme, or helping some high-school kids fill out their college applications. Show them the path that you took. Or you can think a little bigger – you can get your entire congregation or your community to start a mentoring programme; maybe convince your new employer to sponsor scholarships for underprivileged kids. Or maybe you could think a little higher – maybe you could run for school board or Congress, or, yes, even president of the United States.

And then maybe you could build preschools for every single one of our kids. Maybe you could help turn that pipeline to prison into a highway to college; help give every child in America an education that is truly worthy of their promise. Those are the kind of big dreams that folks who founded this university reached for. That is how high they set their bar.

And so we owe it to those folks – the folks who had the audacity to call their little schools 'universities' and name their baby boys 'Emperor' – we owe it to them to reach as high as they did, and to bring others along the way. As the history of this school has taught us, no dream is too big, no vision is too bold; as long as we stay hungry for education and let that hunger be our North Star, there is nothing, graduates, nothing that we cannot achieve.

No dream is too big,
no vision is too bold;
as long as we stay
hungry for education
and let that hunger
be our North Star.

So, graduates, that is your mission. This is your obligation. I want you to keep reaching higher. I want you all to keep raising your bars. Let the next generation know that there is no greater investment than a good education. And if you do all of this, then I am confident that you will uphold that duty and write your own chapter into the legacy of this great university. And let me tell you something, I cannot wait to see the world that your children will be born into.

Congratulations. I love you all. I am honoured to be here. I am proud of you. God bless you. And thank your families.

RIK MAYALL

FIVE MANTRAS

University of Exeter, 2008

adies and gentlemen. Ladies and gentlemen, if I may. Twenty-eight years ago, that man, Paul Jackson, stand up Paul, show them yourself. That's the man. Twenty-eight years ago, that man Paul Jackson walked into a fledgling nightclub in London called The Comedy Store, and asked me if I'd like to be on television. Now that was a very big deal in those days. There were only three channels, so if you went on telly you'd be famous for life, overnight.

So I said yes. Yes please, yes I would like to be on television. So I went along to the BBC, and there in the make-up department I saw the most beautiful woman on the planet. She quickly became my friend, and then my best friend, and then my mistress, and then pregnant, and then my wife, and then the mother of my three children. So Paul, I want to take this rare opportunity to thank you, formally and publicly, for my life.

Right, now to business. Rik Mayall's doctorate. Well, ladies and gentlemen, what can I say? This is extraordinary. This is such an honour, such a joy, such a treat, such a terrible mistake. Now, I have done most things in my long and disgusting life, and I thought I'd done pretty much everything available to me. But I never in my wildest dreams imagined anything like this could happen to me.

I am not a clever person, I'm not a clever person, and I got away with it for a very long time, but now you lot have all caught me. Here I am with all you brainy people, and I'm a man without a brain cell to mention. Yes, I passed my 11 plus exam in 1967. My 11 plus exam in 1967. But everything went downhill from there. I failed seven O-levels. I failed seven O-levels, yes. I failed my maths O-level three times. No, wait. I went on from there, I went on from there to get two F's and a U for my A-levels. F means fail, you guys wouldn't know. The U was for offensive drivel. No, it's true.

But then Manchester University let me in. Yeah, Manchester University let me in on an interview. I mean, they're not up to your standards obviously. They'll take anything up there. But me, uh. I didn't exactly fail my drama degree from Manchester, I just failed to turn up for the exams. It's not that I was too stupid, I was just too drunk, and I was too in bed with girls from the English department.

So here I am, now, Rik Mayall, one 11 plus, three O-levels and a doctorate. I mean …

Doctor Rik Mayall. Unbelievable. I mean, thank you all so much for your imagination and charity. Unbelievable. But, but the celebrations for today aren't for me, they're for you lot. You are the guys who did all the work, and now my young friends is the time to start enjoying your life. Forget about academia, you've done your work. Start

All men are equal, therefore no one can ever be your genuine superior.

celebrating your success, start reaping your rewards, start living your lives to the full in the real, nasty, sexy world out here. Come on, it's time to enjoy yourselves.

Wait. Wait. In return for Exeter's astonishing generosity in making me a doctor, let me give you youngsters a present. Five mantras. Five, no seriously, five mantras to carry with you through your lives. These are mine. These are what have helped me not only to survive, but to be happy. Remember these. Remember these.

All men are equal, therefore ... what are you laughing at? All men, number one, all men are equal, therefore no one can ever be your genuine superior. Number two, it is your future. It is yours to create. Your future is as bright as you make it. Number three, change is a constant of life, so you must never ever lose your wisdom. Your wisdom that you nurtured and enriched here at Exeter University. Number four, if you want to live a full and complete human life, you have to be free. Freedom is paramount. And number five, love is the answer. Love is the answer.

So my friends, there's my present to you. You just make sure you've always got those five things. Equality, opportunity, wisdom, freedom and love. Yeah? Equality, opportunity, wisdom, freedom and love and you'll be all right. You'll be all right with that, and a bit of good luck. So good luck. Congratulations and good luck, my young friends. You get out there and have yourselves a fucking good life.

Bon voyage my young friends, bon voyage.

TIM MINCHIN

———

NINE LIFE LESSONS

University of Western Australia, 2013

I n darker days, I did a corporate gig at a conference for this big company who made and sold accounting software. In a bid, I presume, to inspire their salespeople to greater heights, they'd forked out 12 grand for an inspirational speaker who was this extreme sports dude who had had a couple of his limbs frozen off when he got stuck on a ledge on some mountain. It was weird. Software salespeople need to hear from someone who has had a long, successful and happy career in software sales, not from an overly optimistic, ex-mountaineer. Some poor guy who arrived in the morning hoping to learn about better sales technique ended up going home worried about the blood flow to his extremities. It's not inspirational – it's confusing.

And if the mountain was meant to be a symbol of life's challenges, and the loss of limbs a metaphor for sacrifice, the software guy's not going to get it, is he? Cos he didn't do an arts degree, did he? He should have. Arts degrees are awesome. And they help you find meaning where there is none. And let me assure you, there is none. Don't go looking for it. Searching for meaning is like searching for a rhyme scheme in a cookbook: you won't find it and you'll bugger up your soufflé.

Point being, I'm not an inspirational speaker. I've never lost a limb on a mountainside, metaphorically or otherwise. And I'm certainly not here to give career advice, cos … well I've never really had what most would call a proper job.

However, I have had large groups of people listening to what I say for quite a few years now, and it's given me an inflated sense of self-importance. So I will now – at the ripe old age of 38 – bestow upon you nine life lessons. To echo, of course, the 9 lessons and carols of the traditional Christmas service. Which are also a bit obscure.

You might find some of this stuff inspiring, you will find some of it boring, and you will definitely forget all of it within a week. And be warned, there will be lots of hokey similes, and obscure aphorisms which start well but end up not making sense.

So listen up, or you'll get lost, like a blind man clapping in a pharmacy trying to echo-locate the contact lens fluid.

Here we go:

1. You Don't Have to Have a Dream.
   Americans on talent shows always talk about their dreams. Fine, if you have something that you've always dreamed of, like, in your heart, go for it! After all, it's

I never really had one of these big dreams. And so I advocate passionate dedication to the pursuit of short-term goals. Be micro-ambitious.

something to do with your time ... chasing a dream. And if it's a big enough one, it'll take you most of your life to achieve, so by the time you get to it and are staring into the abyss of the meaninglessness of your achievement, you'll be almost dead so it won't matter.

I never really had one of these big dreams. And so I advocate passionate dedication to the pursuit of short-term goals. Be micro-ambitious. Put your head down and work with pride on whatever is in front of you ... you never know where you might end up. Just be aware that the next worthy pursuit will probably appear in your periphery. Which is why you should be careful of long-term dreams. If you focus too far in front of you, you won't see the shiny thing out the corner of your eye. Right? Good. Advice. Metaphor. Look at me go.

2. Don't Seek Happiness

Happiness is like an orgasm: if you think about it too much, it goes away. Keep busy and aim to make someone else happy, and you might find you get some as a side effect. We didn't evolve to be constantly content. Contented Australophithecus Afarensis got eaten before passing on their genes.

3. Remember, It's All Luck

You are lucky to be here. You were incalculably lucky to be born, and incredibly lucky to be brought up by a nice family that helped you get educated and encouraged you to go to uni. Or if you were born into a horrible family, that's unlucky and you have my sympathy ... but you were still lucky: lucky that you happened to be made of the sort of DNA that made the sort of brain which – when placed in a horrible childhood environment – would make decisions that meant you ended up, eventually, graduating uni. Well done you, for dragging yourself up by the shoelaces, but you were lucky. You didn't create the bit of you that dragged you up. They're not even your shoelaces.

I suppose I worked hard to achieve whatever dubious achievements I've achieved ... but I didn't make the bit of me that works hard, any more than I made the bit of me that ate too many burgers instead of going to lectures while I was here at UWA.

Understanding that you can't truly take credit for your successes, nor truly blame others for their failures will humble you and make you more compassionate.

Empathy is intuitive, but is also something you can work on, intellectually.

4. Exercise

I'm sorry, you pasty, pale, smoking philosophy grads, arching your eyebrows into a Cartesian curve as you watch the Human Movement mob winding their way through the miniature traffic cones of their existence:

you are wrong and they are right. Well, you're half right – you think, therefore you are … but also: you jog, therefore you sleep well, therefore you're not overwhelmed by existential angst. You can't be Kant, and you don't want to be.

Play a sport, do yoga, pump iron, run … whatever … but take care of your body. You're going to need it. Most of you mob are going to live to nearly a hundred, and even the poorest of you will achieve a level of wealth that most humans throughout history could not have dreamed of. And this long, luxurious life ahead of you is going to make you depressed!

But don't despair! There is an inverse correlation between depression and exercise. Do it. Run, my beautiful intellectuals, run. And don't smoke. Natch.

5. Be Hard On Your Opinions

A famous bon mot asserts that opinions are like arseholes, in that everyone has one. There is great wisdom in this … but I would add that opinions differ significantly from arseholes, in that yours should be constantly and thoroughly examined.

We must think critically, and not just about the ideas of others. Be hard on your beliefs. Take them out on to the verandah and beat them with a cricket bat.

Be intellectually rigorous. Identify your biases, your prejudices, your privilege.

Most of society's arguments are kept alive by a failure to acknowledge nuance. We tend to generate false dichotomies, then try to argue one point using two entirely different sets of assumptions, like two tennis players trying to win a match by hitting beautifully executed shots from either end of separate tennis courts.

By the way, while I have science and arts grads in front of me: please don't make the mistake of thinking the arts and sciences are at odds with one another. That is a recent, stupid and damaging idea. You don't have to be unscientific to make beautiful art, to write beautiful things.

If you need proof: Twain, Adams, Vonnegut, McEwan, Sagan, Shakespeare, Dickens. For a start.

You don't need to be superstitious to be a poet. You don't need to hate GM technology to care about the beauty of the planet. You don't have to claim a soul to promote compassion.

Science is not a body of knowledge nor a system of belief; it is just a term which describes humankind's incremental acquisition of understanding through observation. Science is awesome.

The arts and sciences need to work together to improve how knowledge is communicated. The idea that many Australians – including our new PM and my distant cousin Nick – believe that the science of anthropogenic global warming is controversial, is a powerful indicator of the extent of our failure to communicate. The fact that 30 per cent of this room just bristled is further evidence still. The fact that that bristling is more to do with politics than science is even more despairing.

6. Be a Teacher

Please? Please be a teacher. Teachers are the most admirable and important people in the world. You don't have to do it forever, but if you're in doubt about what to do, be an amazing teacher. Just for your twenties. Be a primary-school teacher. Especially if you're a bloke – we need male primary-school teachers. Even if you're not a teacher, be a teacher. Share your ideas. Don't take for granted your education. Rejoice in what you learn, and spray it.

7. Define Yourself By What You Love

I've found myself doing this thing a bit recently, where, if someone asks me what sort of music I like, I say 'well I don't listen to the radio because pop lyrics annoy me'. Or if someone asks me what food I like, I say 'I think truffle oil is overused and slightly obnoxious'. And I see it all the time online, people whose idea of being part of a subculture is to hate Coldplay or football or feminists or the Liberal Party. We have a tendency to define ourselves in opposition to stuff; as a comedian, I make a living out of it. But try to also express your passion for things you love. Be demonstrative and generous in your praise of those you admire. Send thank-you cards and give standing ovations. Be pro-stuff, not just anti-stuff.

8. Respect People With Less Power Than You

I have, in the past, made important decisions about people I work with – agents and producers – based largely on how they treat wait staff in restaurants. I don't care if you're the most powerful cat in the room, I will judge you on how you treat the least powerful. So there.

9. Don't Rush

You don't need to already know what you're going to do with the rest of your life. I'm not saying sit around smoking cones all day, but also, don't panic. Most people I know who were sure of their career path at 20 are having midlife crises now.

I said at the beginning of this ramble that life is meaningless. It was not a flippant assertion. I think it's absurd: the idea of seeking 'meaning' in the set of circumstances that happens to exist after 13.8 billion years' worth of unguided events. Leave it to humans to think the universe has a purpose for them. However,

I am no nihilist. I am not even a cynic. I am, actually, rather romantic. And here's my idea of romance:

You will soon be dead. Life will sometimes seem long and tough and, God, it's tiring. And you will sometimes be happy and sometimes sad. And then you'll be old. And then you'll be dead.

There is only one sensible thing to do with this empty existence, and that is: fill it. Not fillet. Fill. It.

And in my opinion (until I change it), life is best filled by learning as much as you can about as much as you can, taking pride in whatever you're doing, having compassion, sharing ideas, running(!), being enthusiastic. And then there's love, and travel, and wine, and sex, and art, and kids, and giving, and mountain climbing ... but you know all that stuff already.

It's an incredibly exciting thing, this one, meaningless life of yours. Good luck.

Thank you for indulging me.

NORA EPHRON

BE THE HEROINE

Wellesley College, 1996

Presbyterian Walsh, trustees, faculty, friends, noble parents . . . and dear Class of 1996, I am so proud of you.

Thank you for asking me to speak to you today. I had a wonderful time trying to imagine who had been ahead of me on the list and had said no; I was positive you'd have to have gone to Martha Stewart first. And I meant to call her to see what she would have said, but I forgot. She would probably be up here telling you how to turn your lovely black robes into tents. I will try to be at least as helpful, if not quite as specific as that.

I'm very conscious of how easy it is to let people down on a day like this, because I remember my own graduation from Wellesley very, very well, I am sorry to say. The speaker was Santha Rama Rau, who was a woman writer, and I was going to be a woman writer. And in fact, I had spent four years at Wellesley going to lectures by women writers hoping that I would be the beneficiary of some terrific secret – which I never was.

And now here I was at graduation, under these very trees, absolutely terrified. Something was over. Something

107

safe and protected. And something else was about to begin. I was heading off to New York, and I was sure that I would live there forever and never meet anyone and end up dying one of those New York deaths where no one even notices you're missing until the smell drifts into the hallway weeks later. And I sat here thinking, 'OK, Santha, this is my last chance for a really terrific secret, lay it on me,' and she spoke about the need to place friendship over love of country, which I must tell you had never crossed my mind one way or the other.

I want to tell you a little bit about my class, the Class of 1962. When we came to Wellesley in the fall of 1958, there was an article in the *Harvard Crimson* about the women's colleges, one of those stupid mean little articles full of stereotypes, like girls at Bryn Mawr wear black. We were girls then, by the way, Wellesley girls.

How long ago was it? It was so long ago that while I was here, Wellesley actually threw six young women out for lesbianism. It was so long ago that we had curfews. It was so long ago that if you had a boy in your room, you had to leave the door open six inches, and if you closed the door you had to put a sock on the doorknob.

In my class of, I don't know, maybe 375 young women, there were six Asians and five blacks. There was a strict quota on the number of Jews. Tuition was $2,000 a year, and in my junior year it was raised to $2,250, and my parents practically had a heart attack.

How long ago? If you needed an abortion, you drove to a gas station in Union, New Jersey, with $500 in cash in an envelope, and you were taken, blindfolded, to a motel room and operated on without an anaesthetic.

On the lighter side, and as you no doubt read in the *New York Times Magazine*, and were flabbergasted to learn, there were the posture pictures. We not only took off most of our clothes to have our posture pictures taken, we took them off without ever even thinking, 'This is weird, why are we doing this?' –not only that, we had also had speech therapy. I was told I had a New Jersey accent I really ought to do something about, which was a shock to me since I was from Beverly Hills, California, and had never set foot in the state of New Jersey . . . not only that, we were required to take a course called Fundamentals, Fundies, where we actually were taught how to get in and out of the back seat of the car. Some of us were named things like Winkie. We all parted our hair in the middle.

How long ago was it? It was so long ago that among the things that I honestly cannot conceive of life without, that had not yet been invented: panty hose, lattes, Advil, pasta (there was no pasta then, there was only spaghetti and maca-roni) – I sit here writing this speech on a computer next to a touch-tone phone with an answering machine and a Rolodex, there are several CDs on my desk, a bottle of Snapple, there are felt-tip pens and an electric pencil sharpener . . . well, you get the point, it was a long time ago.

Anyway, as I was saying, the *Crimson* had this snippy article which said that Wellesley was a school for Tunicata – Tunicata apparently being small fish who spend the first part of their lives frantically swimming around the ocean floor exploring their environment, and the second part of their lives just lying there breeding. It was mean and snippy, but it had the horrible ring of truth, it was one of those do-not-ask-for-whom-the-bell-tolls things, and it burned itself into our brains. Years later, at my twenty-fifth reunion, one of my classmates mentioned it, and everyone remembered what Tunicata were, word for word.

My class went to college in the era when you got a master's degree in teaching because it was 'something to fall back on' in the worst-case scenario, the worst-case scenario being that no one married you and you actually had to go to work. As this same classmate said at our reunion, 'Our education was a dress rehearsal for a life we never led.' Isn't that the saddest line? We weren't meant to have futures; we were meant to marry them. We weren't meant to have politics, or careers that mattered, or opinions, or lives; we were meant to marry them. If you wanted to be an architect, you married an architect. *Non ministrari sed ministrare* – you know the old joke, not to be ministers but to be ministers' wives.

I've written about my years at Wellesley, and I don't want to repeat myself any more than is necessary. But I do want to retell one anecdote from the piece I did about my tenth Wellesley reunion. I'll tell it a little differently for those of you who read it. Which was that, during my junior year, when I was engaged for a very short period of time, I thought I might transfer to Barnard my senior year. I went to see my class dean and she said to me, 'Let me give you some advice. You've worked so hard at Wellesley, when you marry, take a year off. Devote yourself to your husband and your marriage.'

Of course it was a stunning piece of advice to give me because I'd always intended to work after college. My mother was a career woman, and all of us, her four daughters, grew up understanding that the question, 'What do you want to be when you grow up?' was as valid for girls as for boys. Take a year off being a wife. I always wondered what I was supposed to do in that year. Iron?

I repeated the story for years, as proof that Wellesley wanted its graduates to be merely housewives. But I turned out to be wrong, because years later I met another Wellesley graduate who had been as hell-bent on domesticity as I had been on a career. And she had gone to the same dean with the same problem, and the dean had said to her, 'Don't have children right away. Take a year to work.'

And so I saw that what Wellesley wanted was for us to avoid the extremes. To be instead, that thing in the middle. A lady. We were to take the fabulous education we had received here and use it to preside at dinner table or at a committee meeting, and when two people disagreed we would be intelligent enough to step in and point out the remarkable similarities between their two opposing positions. We were to spend our lives making nice.

Many of my classmates did exactly what they were supposed to when they graduated from Wellesley, and some of them, by the way, lived happily ever after.

But many of them didn't. All sorts of things happened that no one expected. They needed money so they had to work. They got divorced so they had to work. They were bored witless so they had to work. The women's movement came along and made harsh value judgements about their lives – judgements that caught them by surprise, because they were doing what they were supposed to be doing, weren't they? The rules had changed; they were caught in some kind of strange time warp.

They had never intended to be the heroines of their own lives; they'd intended to be – what? – First Ladies, I guess, first ladies in the lives of big men. They ended up feeling like victims. They ended up, and this is really sad, thinking that their years in college were the best years of their lives.

Why am I telling you this? It was a long time ago, right? Things have changed, haven't they? Yes, they have. But I mention it because I want to remind you of the undertow, of the specific gravity. American society has a remarkable ability to resist change, or to take whatever change has taken place and attempt to make it go away.

Things are different for you than they were for us. Just the fact that you chose to come to a single-sex college makes you smarter than we were – we came because it's what you did in those days – and the college you are graduating from is a very different place. All sorts of things caused Wellesley to change, but it did change, and today it's a place that understands its obligations to women in today's world.

The women's movement has made a huge difference, too, particularly for young women like you. There are women doctors and women lawyers. There are anchor-women, although most of them are blonde. But at the same time, the pay differential between men and women has barely changed.

In my business, the movie business, there are many more women directors, but it's just as hard to make a movie about women as it ever was, and look at the parts the Oscar-nominated actresses played this year: hooker, hooker, hooker, hooker and nun. It's 1996, and you are graduating from Wellesley in the Year of the Wonderbra.

The Wonderbra is not a step forward for women. Nothing that hurts that much is a step forward for women. What I'm saying is, don't delude yourself that the powerful cultural values that wrecked the lives of so many of my classmates have vanished from the earth.

Don't let the *New York Times* article about the brilliant success of Wellesley graduates in the business world fool you – there's still a glass ceiling. Don't let the number

Don't underestimate how much antagonism there is towards women and how many people wish we could turn the clock back.

of women in the work force trick you – there are still lots of magazines devoted almost exclusively to making perfect casseroles and turning various things into tents.

Don't underestimate how much antagonism there is towards women and how many people wish we could turn the clock back. One of the things people always say to you if you get upset is, 'Don't take it personally,' but listen hard to what's going on and, please, I beg you, take it personally.

Understand: every attack on Hillary Clinton for not knowing her place is an attack on you. Underneath almost all those attacks are the words: get back, get back to where you once belonged. When Elizabeth Dole pretends that she isn't serious about her career, that is an attack on you. The acquittal of O.J. Simpson is an attack on you. Any move to limit abortion rights is an attack on you – whether or not you believe in abortion. The fact that Clarence Thomas is sitting on the Supreme Court today is an attack on you.

Above all, be the heroine of your life, not the victim. Because you don't have the alibi my class had – this is one of the great achievements and mixed blessings you inherit: unlike us, you can't say nobody told you there were other options. Your education is a dress rehearsal for a life that is yours to lead.

Twenty-five years from now, you won't have as easy a time making excuses as my class did. You won't be able to blame the deans, or the culture, or anyone else: you will

You can't say nobody
told you there were
other options. Your
education is a dress
rehearsal for a life
that is yours to lead.

have no one to blame but yourselves. Whoa. So what are you going to do?

This is the season when a clutch of successful women – who have it all – give speeches to women like you and say: 'To be perfectly honest, you can't have it all.' Maybe young women don't wonder whether they can have it all any longer, but in case any of you are wondering, of course you can have it all. What are you going to do? Everything, is my guess. It will be a little messy, but embrace the mess. It will be complicated, but rejoice in the complications. It will not be anything like what you think it will be like, but surprises are good for you. And don't be frightened: you can always change your mind. I know: I've had four careers and three husbands.

And this is something else I want to tell you, one of the hundreds of things I didn't know when I was sitting here so many years ago: you are not going to be you, fixed and immutable you, forever. We have a game we play when we're waiting for tables in restaurants, where you have to write the five things that describe yourself on a piece of paper.

When I was your age, I would have put: ambitious, Wellesley graduate, daughter, Democrat, single. Ten years later not one of those five things turned up on my list. I was: journalist, feminist, New Yorker, divorced, funny. Today not one of those five things turns up in my list: writer, director, mother, sister, happy.

Whatever those five things are for you today, they won't make the list in ten years – not that you still won't be some of those things, but they won't be the five most important things about you. Which is one of the most delicious things available to women, and more particularly to women than to men. I think. It's slightly easier for us to shift, to change our minds, to take another path. Yogi Berra, the former New York Yankee who made a speciality of saying things that were famously maladroit, quoted himself at a recent commencement speech he gave. 'When you see a fork in the road,' he said, 'take it.' Yes, it's supposed to be a joke, but as someone said in a movie I made, 'Don't laugh, this is my life.' This is the life many women lead: two paths diverge in a wood, and we get to take them both. It's another of the nicest things about being women: we can do that.

Did I say it was hard? Yes, but let me say it again so that none of you can ever say the words, 'Nobody said it was so hard.' But it's also incredibly interesting. You are so lucky to have that life as an option.

Whatever you choose, however many roads you travel, I hope that you choose not to be a lady. I hope you will find some way to break the rules and make a little trouble out there. And I also hope that you will choose to make some of that trouble on behalf of women. Thank you. Good luck. The first act of your life is over. Welcome to the best years of your lives.

SALMAN RUSHDIE

———————

DEFY THE GODS

Bard College, 1996

Members of the Class of 1996, I see in the newspaper that Southampton University on Long Island got Kermit the Frog to give the commencement address this year.

You, unfortunately, have to make do with me. The only Muppet connection I can boast is that my former editor at Alfred Knopf was also the editor of that important self-help text, *Miss Piggy's Guide to Life*. I once asked him how it had been to work with such a major star and he replied, reverentially, 'Salman: the pig was divine.'

In England, where I went to college, we don't do things quite this way on graduation day, so I've been doing a little research into commencement and its traditions. The first American friend I asked told me that in her graduation year – not at this college, I hasten to add – she and her fellow students were so incensed at the choice of commencement speaker – whom I suppose I should not name – oh, all right then, it was Jeane Kirkpatrick – that they boycotted the ceremony and staged a sit-in in one of the college buildings instead. It is a considerable relief, therefore, to note that you are all here.

As for myself, I graduated from Cambridge University in 1968 – the great year of student protest – and I have to tell you that I almost didn't make it.

This story has nothing to do with politics or demonstrations; it is, rather, the improbable and cautionary tale of a thick brown gravy-and-onion sauce.

It begins a few nights before my graduation day, when some anonymous wit chose to redecorate my room, in my absence, by hurling a bucketful of the aforesaid gravy-and-onions all over the walls and furniture, to say nothing of my record player and my clothes.

With that ancient tradition of fairness and justice upon which the colleges of Cambridge pride themselves, my college instantly held me solely responsible for the mess, ignored all my representations to the contrary, and informed me that unless I paid for the damage before the ceremony, I would not be permitted to graduate.

It was the first, but, alas, not the last occasion on which I would find myself wrongly accused of muckspreading. I paid up, I have to report, and was therefore declared eligible to receive my degree; in a defiant spirit, possibly influenced by my recent gravy experience, I went to the ceremony wearing brown shoes, and was promptly plucked out of the parade of my gowned and properly black-shod contemporaries, and ordered back to my quarters to change.

I am not sure why people in brown shoes were deemed to be dressed improperly, but once again I was facing a judgement against which there could be no appeal. Once again, I gave in, sprinted off to change my shoes, got back to the parade in the nick of time; and at length, after these vicissitudes, when my turn came, I was required to hold a university officer by his little finger, and to follow him slowly up to where the vice chancellor sat upon a mighty throne. As instructed, I knelt at his feet, held up my hands, palms together, in a gesture of supplication, and begged in Latin for the degree, for which, I could not help thinking, I had worked extremely hard for three years, supported by my family at considerable expense.

I recall being advised to hold my hands way up above my head, in case the elderly vice chancellor, leaning forward to clutch at them, should topple off his great chair and land on top of me. I did as I was advised; the elderly gentleman did not topple; and, also in Latin, he finally admitted me to the degree of Bachelor of Arts.

Looking back at that day, I am a little appalled by my passivity, hard though it is to see what else I could have done. I could have not paid up, not changed my shoes, not knelt to supplicate for my BA. I preferred to surrender, and get the degree.

I have grown more stubborn since. I have come to the conclusion, which I now offer you, that I was wrong to compromise; wrong to make an accommodation with injustice, no matter how persuasive the reasons. Injustice, today, still conjures up, in my mind, the memory of gravy.

Injustice, for me, is a brown, lumpy, congealing fluid, and it smells pungently, tearfully, of onions. Unfairness is the feeling of running back to your room, flat out, at the last minute, to change your outlawed brown shoes. It is the business of being forced to beg, on your knees, in a dead language, for what is rightfully yours.

This, then, is what I learned on my own graduation day; this is the message I have derived from the parables of the Unknown Gravy-bomber, the Vetoed Footwear and the Unsteady Vice-Chancellor upon his Throne, and which I pass on to you today: first, if, as you go through life, people should some day accuse you of what one might call aggravated gravy abuse – and they will, they will – and if in fact you are innocent of abusing gravy, do not take the rap.

Second: those who would reject you because you are wearing the wrong shoes are not worth being accepted by.

And third: kneel before no man. Stand up for your rights. I like to think that Cambridge University, where I was so happy for three marvellous years, and from which I gained so much – I hope your years at Bard have been as happy, and that you feel you have gained as much – that Cambridge University, with its finely developed British sense of irony, intended me to learn precisely these valuable lessons from the events of that strange graduation day.

Members of the Class of 1996, we are here to celebrate with you one of the great days of your lives. We participate today in the rite of passage by which you are released from this life of preparation into that life for which you are now as prepared as anyone ever is.

As you stand at the gate of the future, I should like to share with you a piece of information about the extraordinary institution you are leaving, which will explain the reason why it is such a particular pleasure for me to be with you today. In 1989, within weeks of the threat made against me by the mullahs of Iran, I was approached by the president of Bard, through my literary agent, and asked if I would consider accepting a place on the faculty of this college. More than a place; I was assured that I could find, here in Annandale, among the Bard community, many friends, and a safe haven in which I could live and work.

Alas, I was not able, in those difficult days, to take up this courageous offer, but I have never forgotten that at a moment when red-alert signals were flashing all over the world, and all sorts of people and institutions were running scared, Bard College did the opposite – that it moved towards me, in intellectual solidarity and human concern, and made, not lofty speeches, but a concrete offer of help.

I hope you will all feel proud that Bard, quietly, without fanfares, made such a principled gesture at such a time. I am certainly extremely proud to be a recipient of Bard's honorary degree, and to have been accorded the exceptional privilege of addressing you today.

Hubris, according to the Greeks, was the sin of defying the gods, and could, if you were really unlucky, unleash against you the terrifying, avenging figure of the goddess Nemesis, who carried in one hand an apple bough and, in the other, the Wheel of Fortune, which would one day circle round to the inevitable moment of vengeance.

As I have been, in my time, accused not only of gravy abuse and wearing brown shoes but of hubris, too, and since I have come to believe that such defiance is an inevitable and essential aspect of what we call freedom, I thought I might commend it to you.

For in the years to come you will find yourselves up against gods of all sorts, big and little gods, corporate and incorporeal gods, all of them demanding to be worshipped and obeyed – the myriad deities of money and power, of convention and custom, that will seek to limit and control your thoughts and lives. Defy them; that's my advice to you. Thumb your noses; cock your snooks. For, as the myths tell us, it is by defying the gods that human beings have best expressed their humanity.

The Greeks tell many stories of quarrels between us and the gods. Arachne, the great artist of the loom, sets her skills of weaving and embroidery against those of the goddess of wisdom herself, Minerva or Pallas Athene; and impudently chooses to weave versions of only those scenes which reveal the mistakes and weaknesses of the gods – the

Defiance is an inevitable and essential aspect of what we call freedom.

rape of Europa, Leda and the Swan. For this – for the irreverence, not for her lesser skill – for what we would now call art, and chutzpah – the goddess changes her mortal rival into a spider.

Queen Niobe of Thebes tells her people not to worship Latona, the mother of Diana and Apollo, saying 'What folly is this! – To prefer beings whom you never saw to those who stand before your eyes!' For this sentiment, which today we would call humanism, the gods murder her children and husband, and she metamorphoses into a rock, petrified with grief, from which there trickles an unending river of tears.

Prometheus the Titan steals fire from the gods and gives it to mankind. For this – for what we would now call the desire for progress, for improved scientific and technological capabilities – he is bound to a rock while a great bird gnaws eternally at his liver, which regenerates as it is consumed.

The interesting point is that the gods do not come out of these stories at all well. If Arachne is overly proud when she seeks to compete with a goddess, it is only an artist's pride, joined to the gutsiness of youth; whereas Minerva, who could afford to be gracious, is merely vindictive. The story increases Arachne's shadow, as they say, and diminishes Minerva's. It is Arachne who gains, from the tale, a measure of immortality. And the cruelty of the gods to the family of Niobe proves her point.

Who could prefer the rule of such cruel gods to self-rule, the rule of men and women by men and women, however flawed that may be? Once again, the gods are weakened by their show of strength, while the human beings grow stronger, even though – even as – they are destroyed. And tormented Prometheus, of course, Prometheus with his gift of fire, is the greatest hero of all.

It is men and women who have made the world, and they have made it in spite of their gods. The message of the myths is not the one the gods would have us learn – that we should behave ourselves and know our place – but its exact opposite. It is that we must be guided by our natures. Our worst natures can, it's true, be arrogant, venal, corrupt or selfish; but in our best selves, we – that is, you – can and will be joyous, adventurous, cheeky, creative, inquisitive, demanding, competitive, loving and defiant.

Do not bow your heads. Do not know your place. Defy the gods. You will be astonished how many of them turn out to have feet of clay. Be guided, if possible, by your better natures. Great good luck and many congratulations to you all.

DR JOANNE LIU

ON IMPERFECTION

Barnard College, 2017

Thank you, President Goldberg, distinguished members of the Board of Trustees, esteemed faculty members, proud parents, siblings and friends.

It is a wonderful, humbling honour to be with you today.

And to the Barnard Class of 2017: CONGRATULATIONS!! You made it! You have every right to be proud. So, do remember to celebrate! Celebrate your achievement. You deserve it.

I hope you will also remember this: your educational accomplishments, just like your achievements to follow, are not because you are perfect.

Despite what your parents may have told you, I'm here to tell you how imperfect you are. How imperfect we all are. Including me.

Imperfection is what makes us human, and actually capable of achieving so much. It's what we do with our imperfections – our acceptance of them – that determines our course in life.

For you, life in many ways begins now. You are leaving the comfortable and supportive confines of the academy, and entering a world of uncertainty.

Imperfection is what makes us human, and actually capable of achieving so much.

You are also entering a world of promise, and of firsts. For many of you, following this first university success, your first jobs await. Perhaps your first true loves, callings, first real challenges, joys – and, yes, first true disappointments. Even your first failures or setbacks.

Despair not.

While your firsts are never perfect, they will define and direct you. This is a first for me today. My first time at Radio City Music Hall. Delivering my first commencement speech no less.

I was invited to deliver these remarks in the wake of the election in November. I hesitated before agreeing, overwhelmed by the honour and the responsibility.

To reassure me, I was told by someone within the Barnard administration: 'We are overwhelmingly enthusiastic about honouring you and your work. Our past speakers include Barack Obama, Hillary Clinton and Samantha Power, so you would be in good company.'

No pressure whatsoever.

I admit to having panic attacks since then.

I watched all the commencement speeches at Barnard that I could. I bought books on how to write commencement speeches. I even watched TED Talks. Here's what I came up with:

I grew up in a 1970s French-speaking suburb of Quebec City. There were four other Chinese families in town. Two were my uncles' families. The other two ran competing Chinese restaurants.

I was a visible minority growing up. I knew I was Chinese before knowing I was a woman.

I collected hockey cards and dreamed of being a hockey player.

I could have been labelled 'gender fluid'.

The youngest of four, I went to French school, while my siblings went to English school, along with most other children of immigrants.

While my school choice was one of integration, it meant I had no big sister or brother to protect me.

After my first day of school, having left the protective cocoon of home, I returned with a bloody face. Some kids had punched me, accusing me of having a flat nose.

I sobbed before my mother.

Now, I belong to a family in which caring is displayed through toughness.

My mother stared at me for a few seconds. Then she solemnly declared that my nose was indeed flat.

I picked myself up and washed my face.

A first had occurred. And it was a fundamental life lesson.

I was out in the world now.

Imperfection, even in the form of a flat nose, is an occurrence and fact of life. It happens.

Never apologize for what or who you are. Never feel sorry for yourself.

Never apologize for what or who you are. Never feel sorry for yourself.

Perhaps like many of you here today, I found my first inspiration in the pages of a book. As a teenager, I read *The Plague*, by Albert Camus – a book that changed my life. The novel's protagonist, Dr Rieux, has very little to offer the dying all around him. Yet he persists.

'Why are you so dedicated?' he's asked.

He answers: 'Quite simply, I am still not used to seeing people die.'

From that moment on, I promised myself to fight for life. Death indeed matters, and is not something to become accustomed to.

I was also inspired by the biography of a physician working in Afghanistan with Doctors Without Borders – also known as Médecins Sans Frontières, or MSF.

It was then that I decided to become a doctor.

Several years later, when I told my father about my acceptance to medical school, he replied:

'Too much education, you will never find a husband.'

It didn't stop me.

For the next 15 years, I based all my educational choices on developing skills I could use at the front line – from paediatrics to paediatric emergency training, including here in New York, at Bellevue Hospital.

My first field assignment was in 1996 in Mauritania, in northern Africa. I was the only physician in a camp of 40,000 refugees from Mali.

A United Nations officer, approaching the end of his assignment, wanted to move the camp closer to the border before he left – to demonstrate that he had done something – anything – to get the refugees closer to home.

But it was during the rainy season. I objected forcefully, and reported the plan to my headquarters in Paris.

Nothing happened.

People squatted for days under heavy rains, without shelter. Many became sick.

I was shattered, and kept asking myself: 'This is humanitarianism?'

I resigned in protest. It was the only thing I could do.

So, my assignment was shortened to three months. I agreed to wait for my replacement – I'm a responsible quitter, after all.

And it was an imperfect decision in so many ways.

Imagine: a dream carried within for 15 years, ultimately reduced to bitter confusion and disappointment.

I could have succumbed and ditched my dream of a lifetime.

Instead, I went to Sri Lanka a few weeks later, and on to multiple other assignments thereafter.

Be assured that each field posting featured its own disappointments and shortcomings – its own imperfections. But also, at times, they were the perfect incarnation of our common humanity.

Be it a severely malnourished child brought back from the brink; a father walking again after a leg amputation; a woman, who could otherwise die during childbirth, safely delivering a baby.

So, accept the disappointments in life, for there will be many. But push through them stubbornly, so that you may find what balances them: the successes, the joys, the opportunities to contribute – and to make a difference.

In 2006, after several years in the field, I sought election as the international president of Doctors Without Borders.

I lost. And I was devastated.

I began to doubt myself, my drive and what I had to offer.

One must expose oneself when aspiring to any leadership role – to become vulnerable.

And I remained hung up on the defeat for years.

Until one day, when someone told me to snap out of it.

Very few people, of course, get elected president the first time around.

Well, I suppose there are exceptions …

It took seven years to again find the conviction that I had something to offer – with all my imperfections – in a leadership role with MSF.

In 2013, I had the immense privilege to be elected international president.

It happened just as the conflict in Syria was escalating, and right before the devastating Ebola outbreak in West Africa.

Beyond the massive responsibility, being the voice of a 35,000-person workforce – and of our patients – presented another very humbling 'first' in life, for which there is no instruction manual.

I vividly remember my first press conference at the United Nations in Geneva, upon my return from visiting the Ebola-affected countries in West Africa.

The flight was delayed by heavy tropical rains, and I landed in Geneva just a couple of hours before the scheduled conference.

Sleep-deprived, and feeling quite intimidated, I faced the swarming media to talk about what I had just seen.

And I remember so well the email my husband sent to me after I delivered the briefing:

'My love, you are the only person I know who has subtitles when you speak in French, and when you speak in English.'

So much for my self-confidence. My own, permanent imperfection, for all the world to see.

So be it.

But within the Ebola experience lie broader, core life lessons. In the face of the world's indifference, my colleagues and I were forced to turn back sick and dying people for lack of bed space in our treatment centres.

We scaled up, constantly asking ourselves: 'How far can we go, how long will we last?' Despite the loss of patients, the loss of colleagues and despite being so lost in our losses, we persevered.

Ultimately, though, our medical teams confronted me directly, telling me that if the world did not show up, MSF should leave.

I promised Liberia's president, Ellen Johnson Sirleaf, that although we were stretched to the breaking point, we would try to do more, and that I would use my voice and position to alert the world to what was happening.

When I briefed the United Nations General Assembly in September 2014, I admitted MSF's failure to tackle the pandemic.

I issued a desperate, exceptional plea, asking the world to deploy civilian and military assets to West Africa to stem Ebola's tide.

MSF was portrayed as the poster child of the Ebola epidemic response. The perfect heroes.

Far from it.

At the level of patient care, we lamentably failed. In unchartered territory, we ultimately failed in the standard of care we could provide.

We had to settle for imperfection, because imperfection was better than no care at all.

It meant medical care stripped to its bare bones. At best, it was rudimentary palliative care. At worst, we gave people a cot to die upon – maybe. Some didn't have even that.

Certainly, we made some difference for many – but our offering was ultimately imperfect.

While hopefully not to this extreme, you too will face these moments. And you too will have to settle for less than perfect. It's what you do with the imperfections that matter.

Despite our flaws and imperfect offerings, we stood by our patients – even if we weren't making a huge medical difference.

And so here you are, graduating from Barnard. You're regarded as golden, with so much opportunity ahead. With so many hopes and expectations vested in you.

That's a lot of pressure.

That's a lot to live up to.

It may not be the same as treating a dying patient, but it's no less significant.

You don't have to be perfect. You just have to do your best.

And the reality is that your best may be imperfect. And that's OK.

Because our imperfect offerings set us on a path towards improvement, adaptation, creativity, perseverance and hard work. And towards humility. For perfection is an elusive pursuit.

Acknowledging and embracing your limits, indeed some of your imperfections, is an act of grace. Don't let anyone tell you otherwise.

There are also imperfect choices. A short time ago, I was among refugees and migrants on the Greek island of Samos. Most had come from Syria, Afghanistan and Iraq.

After fleeing for their lives to Europe, they found themselves effectively trapped on the island, with no idea of what the future would hold.

A colleague told me a story about a Syrian mother and her three children. She became separated from her husband after they fled Syria and she assumed he was dead. Her family now lives clandestinely to avoid being sent back where they came from.

During one conversation, the mother mentioned something about a fourth child. My colleague said to her, 'I thought you only had three children.'

The woman then opened up.

She paid a smuggler to send her fourth child, a 14-year-old girl, to Germany. She played the odds, putting her daughter at extreme risk to try to save her, and by extension her family. If the daughter made it, reunification in Germany could be possible.

We know the reality her daughter could face. She could be abused. She could be trafficked. She could be raped. And her mother is not naïve. She knows all this, too.

These are the so-called 'choices' people make, when there really are no choices at all. Being the daughter of an immigrant family, I know that the motivations for migrant parents to offer a future for their children are unshakeable, unbeatable.

No one sets out through hell like this for no reason.

No one puts their children on flimsy rubber boats on a perilous sea, unless there is no other choice.

No one sends them off with strangers to save them, unless they are forced to.

And so, what does all this mean for you? You, who are so blessed with opportunity and freedom. And with real choices. At times, the blessing of your choices may feel like a curse.

Do not lose yourself in chasing so-called perfect decisions and perfect solutions. For there are none.

Don't become paralysed by the quest for perfection.

You may have to accept setbacks, but do not be undone by them. Always remind yourself that every problem, every complex situation, has a solution – as imperfect as it may be.

And, always choose action.

It is not enough to say that something is unacceptable. Bad policies, injustices and violations will still move forward in the face of choosing not to act.

If something is unacceptable to you, go beyond just saying so. Or resending a tweet that says so. Words bereft of action are just that: words.

I learned that Barnard has declared itself a migrant sanctuary. Bravo. Now what are you going to do about it?

For we are indeed in a time when the welfare of human beings is not necessarily placed at the centre of policy and government action. And this forces a fundamental question we must all ask ourselves:

How do we preserve our humanity?

Wherever you end up: the corner office; the hospital ward; the board room; the trading floor; the classroom; the performance stage; or the government agency – always ask yourself that question.

If I may, I'd like to return briefly to the Ebola outbreak. It serves as a meaningful metaphor.

The world ultimately acted when our own ways of life in the West appeared threatened, after so many had already needlessly perished.

Think about that.

If we only assist others when we think our own interests are at stake, we'll likely have acted too late.

But if we choose to act out of the belief and basic logic that our own well-being is intertwined with – and dependent upon – the well-being of others, we will make better choices.

Not perfect, but better.

Parents, you have raised brilliantly imperfect daughters in this Class of 2017. And you daughters now belong to an educated elite. But an elite with responsibilities.

Among your responsibilities is to own your imperfections, without apology or shame.

Because imperfection makes us crave more.

It also keeps us humble.

But first and foremost, imperfection grants us our humanity.

I have worked in the most modern medical facilities and in the most challenging war zones and epidemics; in world-class emergency rooms, and in isolated, forsaken refugee camps.

People always ask me: 'What drives you? Aren't you tired of those hopeless situations with no perfect solutions?'

My answer never changes: 'No.'

My colleagues and I work for people who have no choice. And we try to give them our best. It is through action based on need and nothing else that we confront the imperfections of our world.

By giving. Not always perfectly, but by giving nonetheless. Faced with so many choices, you all are uniquely positioned to give.

So, Class of 2017: my warmest congratulations to you. Be proud, live fully in this moment of true achievement. You deserve it.

Then get out there and be brilliantly imperfect.

Thank you.

BARACK OBAMA

FLIP THE SCRIPT

Howard University, 2016

PRESIDENT BARACK OBAMA: Thank you! Hello, Howard! H-U!

AUDIENCE: You know!

OBAMA: H-U!

AUDIENCE: You know!

OBAMA: Thank you so much, everybody. Please, please, have a seat. Oh, I feel important now. Got a degree from Howard. Cicely Tyson said something nice about me.

AUDIENCE MEMBER: I love you, President!

OBAMA: I love you back.

To President Frederick, the Board of Trustees, faculty and staff, fellow recipients of honorary degrees, thank you for the honour of spending this day with you. And congratulations to the Class of 2016! Four years ago, back when you were just freshmen, I understand many of you came by my house the night I was re-elected. So I decided to return the favour and come by yours.

To the parents, the grandparents, aunts, uncles, brothers, sisters, all the family and friends who stood by this class, cheered them on, helped them get here today – this is your day, as well. Let's give them a big round of applause, as well.

I'm not trying to stir up any rivalries here; I just want to see who's in the house. We got Quad? Annex. Drew. Carver. Slow. Towers. And Meridian. Rest in peace, Meridian. Rest in peace.

I know you're all excited today. You might be a little tired, as well. Some of you were up all night making sure your credits were in order. Some of you stayed up too late, ended up at HoChi at 2am. Got some mambo sauce on your fingers.

But you got here. And you've all worked hard to reach this day. You've shuttled between challenging classes and Greek life. You've led clubs, played an instrument or a sport. You volunteered, you interned. You held down one, two, maybe three jobs. You've made lifelong friends and discovered exactly what you're made of. The 'Howard Hustle' has strengthened your sense of purpose and ambition.

Which means you're part of a long line of Howard graduates. Some are on this stage today. Some are in the audience. That spirit of achievement and special responsibility has defined this campus ever since the Freedman's Bureau established Howard just four years after the Emancipation Proclamation; just two years after the Civil War came to an end. They created this university with a vision – a vision of uplift; a vision for an America where our fates would be determined not by our race, gender, religion or creed, but where we would be free – in every sense – to pursue our individual and collective dreams.

It is that spirit that's made Howard a centrepiece of African-American intellectual life and a central part of our larger American story. This institution has been the home of many firsts: the first black Nobel Peace Prize winner. The first black Supreme Court justice. But its mission has been to ensure those firsts were not the last. Countless scholars, professionals, artists and leaders from every field received their training here. The generations of men and women who walked through this yard helped reform our government, cure disease, grow a black middle class, advance civil rights, shape our culture. The seeds of change – for all Americans – were sown here. And that's what I want to talk about today.

As I was preparing these remarks, I realized that when I was first elected president, most of you – the Class of 2016 – were just starting high school. Today, you're graduating college. I used to joke about being old. Now I realize I'm old. It's not a joke any more.

But seeing all of you here gives me some perspective. It makes me reflect on the changes that I've seen over my own lifetime. So let me begin with what may sound like a controversial statement – a hot take.

Given the current state of our political rhetoric and debate, let me say something that may be controversial, and that is this: America is a better place today than it was when I graduated from college. Let me repeat: America is by almost every measure better than it was when I graduated from college. It also happens to be better off than when I took office but that's a longer story. That's a different discussion for another speech.

But think about it. I graduated in 1983. New York City, America's largest city, where I lived at the time, had endured a decade marked by crime and deterioration and near bankruptcy. And many cities were in similar shape. Our nation had gone through years of economic stagnation, the stranglehold of foreign oil, a recession where unemployment nearly scraped 11 per cent. The auto industry was getting its clock cleaned by foreign competition. And don't even get me started on the clothes and the hairstyles. I've tried to eliminate all photos of me from this period. I thought I looked good. I was wrong.

Since that year – since the year I graduated – the poverty rate is down. Americans with college degrees, that rate is up. Crime rates are down. America's cities have undergone a renaissance. There are more women in the workforce. They're earning more money. We've cut teen pregnancy in half. We've slashed the African American dropout rate by almost 60 per cent, and all of you have a computer in your pocket that gives you the world at the touch of a button. In 1983, I was part of fewer than 10 per cent of African Americans who graduated with a bachelor's degree. Today, you're part of the more than 20 per cent who will. And more than half of blacks say we're better off than our parents were at our age – and that our kids will be better off, too.

So America is better. And the world is better, too. A wall came down in Berlin. An Iron Curtain was torn asunder. The obscenity of apartheid came to an end. A young generation in Belfast and London have grown up without ever having to think about IRA bombings. In just the past 16 years, we've come from a world without marriage equality to one where it's a reality in nearly two dozen countries. Around the world, more people live in democracies. We've lifted more than 1 billion people from extreme poverty. We've cut the child mortality rate worldwide by more than half.

America is better. The world is better. And stay with me now – race relations are better since I graduated. That's the truth. No, my election did not create a post-racial society. I don't know who was propagating that notion. That was not mine. But the election itself – and the subsequent one – because the first one, folks might have made a mistake. The second one, they knew what they were getting. The election itself was just one indicator of how attitudes had changed.

In my inaugural address, I remarked that just 60 years earlier, my father might not have been served in a D.C. restaurant – at least not certain of them. There were no black CEOs of Fortune 500 companies. Very few black judges. Shoot, as Larry Wilmore pointed out last week, a lot of folks didn't even think blacks had the tools to be a quarterback. Today, former Bull Michael Jordan isn't just the greatest basketball player of all time – he owns the team. When I was graduating, the main black hero on TV was Mr T. Rap and hip hop were counterculture, underground. Now, Shonda Rhimes owns Thursday night, and Beyoncé runs the world. We're no longer only entertainers, we're producers, studio executives. No longer small business owners – we're CEOs, we're mayors, representatives, presidents of the United States.

I am not saying gaps do not persist. Obviously, they do. Racism persists. Inequality persists. Don't worry – I'm going to get to that. But I wanted to start, Class of 2016, by opening your eyes to the moment that you are in. If you had to choose one moment in history in which you could be born, and you didn't know ahead of time who you were going to be – what nationality, what gender, what race, whether you'd be rich or poor, gay or straight, what faith you'd be born into – you wouldn't choose 100 years ago. You wouldn't choose the fifties, or the sixties, or the seventies. You'd choose right now. If you had to choose a time to be, in the words of Lorraine Hansberry, 'young, gifted and black' in America, you would choose right now.

I tell you all this because it's important to note progress. Because to deny how far we've come would do a disservice to the cause of justice, to the legions of foot soldiers; to not only the incredibly accomplished individuals who have already been mentioned, but your mothers and your dads, and grandparents and great-grandparents, who marched and toiled and suffered and overcame to make this day possible. I tell you this not to lull you into complacency, but to spur you into action – because there's still so much more work to do, so many more miles to travel. And America needs you to gladly, happily take up that work. You all have some work to do. So enjoy the party, because you're going to be busy.

Yes, our economy has recovered from crisis stronger than almost any other in the world. But there are folks of all races who are still hurting – who still can't find work that pays enough to keep the lights on, who still can't save for retirement. We've still got a big racial gap in economic opportunity. The overall unemployment rate is 5 per cent, but the black unemployment rate is almost nine. We've still got an achievement gap when black boys and girls graduate high school and college at lower rates than white boys and white girls. Harriet Tubman may be going on the twenty, but we've still got a gender gap when a black woman working full-time still earns just 66 per cent of what a white man gets paid.

We've got a justice gap when too many black boys and girls pass through a pipeline from underfunded schools to overcrowded jails. This is one area where things have gotten worse. When I was in college, about half a million people in America were behind bars. Today, there are about 2.2 million. Black men are about six times likelier to be in prison right now than white men.

Around the world, we've still got challenges to solve that threaten everybody in the twenty-first century – old scourges like disease and conflict, but also new challenges, from terrorism and climate change.

So make no mistake, Class of 2016 – you've got plenty of work to do. But as complicated and sometimes intractable as these challenges may seem, the truth is that your generation is better positioned than any before you to meet those challenges, to flip the script.

Now, how you do that, how you meet these challenges, how you bring about change will ultimately be up to you. My generation, like all generations, is too confined by our own experience, too invested in our own biases, too stuck in our ways to provide much of the new thinking that will be required. But us old-heads have learned a few things that might be useful in your journey. So with the rest of my time, I'd like to offer some suggestions for how young leaders like you can fulfil your destiny and shape our

There's no
straitjacket, there's
no constraints,
there's no litmus test
for authenticity.

collective future – bend it in the direction of justice and equality and freedom.

First of all – and this should not be a problem for this group – be confident in your heritage. Be confident in your blackness. One of the great changes that's occurred in our country since I was your age is the realization there's no one way to be black. Take it from somebody who's seen both sides of debate about whether I'm black enough. In the past couple months, I've had lunch with the Queen of England and hosted Kendrick Lamar in the Oval Office. There's no straitjacket, there's no constraints, there's no litmus test for authenticity.

Look at Howard. One thing most folks don't know about Howard is how diverse it is. When you arrived here, some of you were like, oh, they've got black people in Iowa? But it's true – this class comes from big cities and rural communities, and some of you crossed oceans to study here. You shatter stereotypes. Some of you come from a long line of Bison. Some of you are the first in your family to graduate from college. You all talk different, you all dress different. You're Lakers fans, Celtics fans, maybe even some hockey fans.

And because of those who've come before you, you have models to follow. You can work for a company, or start your own. You can go into politics, or run an organization that holds politicians accountable. You can write a book that wins the National Book Award, or you can write the new run of *Black Panther*. Or, like one of your alumni, Ta-Nehisi Coates, you can go ahead and just do both. You can create your own style, set your own standard of beauty, embrace your own sexuality. Think about an icon we just lost – Prince. He blew up categories. People didn't know what Prince was doing. And folks loved him for it.

You need to have the same confidence. Or as my daughters tell me all the time, 'You be you, Daddy.' Sometimes Sasha puts a variation on it – 'You do you, Daddy.' And because you're a black person doing whatever it is that you're doing, that makes it a black thing. Feel confident.

Second, even as we each embrace our own beautiful, unique and valid versions of our blackness, remember the tie that does bind us as African Americans – and that is our particular awareness of injustice and unfairness and struggle. That means we cannot sleepwalk through life. We cannot be ignorant of history. We can't meet the world with a sense of entitlement. We can't walk by a homeless man without asking why a society as wealthy as ours allows that state of affairs to occur. We can't just lock up a low-level dealer without asking why this boy, barely out of childhood, felt he had no other options. We have cousins and uncles and brothers and sisters who we remember were just as smart and just as talented as we were, but somehow got ground down by structures that are unfair and unjust.

And that means we have to not only question the world as it is, and stand up for those African Americans who haven't been so lucky – because, yes, you've worked hard, but you've also been lucky. That's a pet peeve of mine: people who have been successful and don't realize they've been lucky. That God may have blessed them; it wasn't nothing you did. So don't have an attitude. But we must expand our moral imaginations to understand and empathize with all people who are struggling, not just black folks who are struggling – the refugee, the immigrant, the rural poor, the transgender person and yes, the middle-aged white guy who you may think has all the advantages, but over the last several decades has seen his world upended by economic and cultural and technological change, and feels powerless to stop it. You got to get in his head, too.

Number three: you have to go through life with more than just passion for change; you need a strategy. I'll repeat that. I want you to have passion, but you have to have a strategy. Not just awareness, but action. Not just hashtags, but votes.

You see, change requires more than righteous anger. It requires a programme, and it requires organizing. At the 1964 Democratic Convention, Fannie Lou Hamer

Passion is vital, but you've got to have a strategy.

– all five-feet-four-inches tall – gave a fiery speech on the national stage. But then she went back home to Mississippi and organized cotton pickers. And she didn't have the tools and technology where you can whip up a movement in minutes. She had to go door to door. And I'm so proud of the new guard of black civil rights leaders who understand this. It's thanks in large part to the activism of young people like many of you, from Black Twitter to Black Lives Matter, that America's eyes have been opened – white, black, Democrat, Republican – to the real problems, for example, in our criminal justice system.

But to bring about structural change, lasting change, awareness is not enough. It requires changes in law, changes in custom. If you care about mass incarceration, let me ask you: how are you pressuring members of Congress to pass the criminal justice reform bill now pending before them? If you care about better policing, do you know who your district attorney is? Do you know who your state's attorney general is? Do you know the difference? Do you know who appoints the police chief and who writes the police training manual? Find out who they are, what their responsibilities are. Mobilize the community, present them with a plan, work with them to bring about change, hold them accountable if they do not deliver. Passion is vital, but you've got to have a strategy.

And your plan better include voting – not just some of the time, but all the time. It is absolutely true that 50 years after the Voting Rights Act, there are still too many barriers in this country to vote. There are too many people trying to erect new barriers to voting. This is the only advanced democracy on earth that goes out of its way to make it difficult for people to vote. And there's a reason for that. There's a legacy to that.

But let me say this: even if we dismantled every barrier to voting, that alone would not change the fact that America has some of the lowest voting rates in the free world. In 2014, only 36 per cent of Americans turned out to vote in the midterms – the second lowest participation rate on record. Youth turnout – that would be you – was less than 20 per cent. Less than 20 per cent. Four out of five did not vote. In 2012, nearly two in three African Americans turned out. And then, in 2014, only two in five turned out. You don't think that made a difference in terms of the Congress I've got to deal with? And then people are wondering, well, how come Obama hasn't gotten this done? How come he didn't get that done? You don't think that made a difference? What would have happened if you had turned out at 50, 60, 70 per cent, all across this country? People try to make this political thing really complicated. Like, what kind of reforms do we need? And how do we need to do that? You know what, just vote. It's math. If you have more votes than the other guy, you get to do what you want. It's not that complicated.

And you don't have excuses. You don't have to guess the number of jelly beans in a jar or bubbles on a bar of soap to register to vote. You don't have to risk your life to cast a ballot. Other people already did that for you. Your grandparents, your great-grandparents might be here today if they were working on it. What's your excuse? When we don't vote, we give away our power, disenfranchise ourselves – right when we need to use the power that we have; right when we need your power to stop others from taking away the vote and rights of those more vulnerable than you are – the elderly and the poor, the formerly incarcerated trying to earn their second chance.

So you got to vote all the time, not just when it's cool, not just when it's time to elect a president, not just when you're inspired. It's your duty. When it's time to elect a member of Congress or a city councilman, or a school board member, or a sheriff. That's how we change our politics – by electing people at every level who are representative of and accountable to us. It is not that complicated. Don't make it complicated.

And finally, change requires more than just speaking out – it requires listening, as well. In particular, it requires listening to those with whom you disagree, and being prepared to compromise. When I was a state senator, I helped pass Illinois's first racial profiling law, and one of the first laws in the nation requiring the videotaping of confessions in capital cases. And we were successful because, early on, I engaged law enforcement. I didn't say to them, oh, you guys are so racist, you need to do something. I understood, as many of you do, that the overwhelming majority of police officers are good, and honest, and courageous, and fair, and love the communities they serve.

And we knew there were some bad apples, and that even the good cops with the best of intentions – including, by the way, African American police officers – might have unconscious biases, as we all do. So we engaged and we listened, and we kept working until we built consensus. And because we took the time to listen, we crafted legislation that was good for the police – because it improved the trust and cooperation of the community – and it was good for the communities, who were less likely to be treated unfairly. And I can say this unequivocally: without at least the acceptance of the police organizations in Illinois, I could never have gotten those bills passed. Very simple. They would have blocked them.

The point is, you need allies in a democracy. That's just the way it is. It can be frustrating and it can be slow. But history teaches us that the alternative to democracy is always worse. That's not just true in this country. It's not a black or white thing. Go to any country where the give and take of democracy has been repealed by one-party rule, and I will show you a country that does not work.

And democracy requires compromise, even when you are 100 per cent right. This is hard to explain sometimes. You can be completely right, and you still are going to have to engage folks who disagree with you. If you think that the only way forward is to be as uncompromising as possible, you will feel good about yourself, you will enjoy a certain moral purity, but you're not going to get what you want. And if you don't get what you want long enough, you will eventually think the whole system is rigged. And that will lead to more cynicism, and less participation, and a downward spiral of more injustice and more anger and more despair. And that's never been the source of our progress. That's how we cheat ourselves of progress.

We remember Dr King's soaring oratory, the power of his letter from a Birmingham jail, the marches he led. But he also sat down with President Johnson in the Oval Office to try and get a Civil Rights Act and a Voting Rights Act passed. And those two seminal bills were not perfect – just like the Emancipation Proclamation was a war document as much as it was some clarion call for freedom. Those mileposts of our progress were not perfect. They did not make up for centuries of slavery or Jim Crow or eliminate racism or provide for 40 acres and a mule. But they made things better. And you know what, I will take better every time. I always tell my staff – better is good, because you consolidate your gains and then you move on to the next fight from a stronger position.

Brittany Packnett, a member of the Black Lives Matter movement and Campaign Zero, one of the Ferguson protest organizers, she joined our Task Force on 21st Century Policing. Some of her fellow activists questioned whether she should participate. She rolled up her sleeves and sat at the same table with big city police chiefs and prosecutors. And because she did, she ended up shaping many of the recommendations of that task force. And those recommendations are now being adopted across the country – changes that many of the protesters called for. If young activists like Brittany had refused to participate out of some sense of ideological purity, then those great ideas would have just remained ideas. But she did participate. And that's how change happens.

America is big and it is boisterous and it is more diverse than ever. The president told me that we've got a significant Nepalese contingent here at Howard. I would not have guessed that. Right on. But it just tells you how interconnected we're becoming. And with so many folks from so many places, converging, we are not always going to agree with each other.

Another Howard alum, Zora Neale Hurston, once said – this is a good quote here: 'Nothing that God ever made is the same thing to more than one person.' Think about that. That's why our democracy gives us a process designed for us to settle our disputes with argument and ideas and votes instead of violence and simple majority rule.

So don't try to shut folks out, don't try to shut them down, no matter how much you might disagree with them. There's been a trend around the country of trying to get colleges to disinvite speakers with a different point of view, or disrupt a politician's rally. Don't do that – no matter how ridiculous or offensive you might find the things that come out of their mouths. Because as my grandmother used to tell me, every time a fool speaks, they are just advertising their own ignorance. Let them talk. Let them talk. If you don't, you just make them a victim, and then they can avoid accountability.

That doesn't mean you shouldn't challenge them. Have the confidence to challenge them, the confidence in the rightness of your position. There will be times when you shouldn't compromise your core values, your integrity, and you will have the responsibility to speak up in the face of injustice. But listen. Engage. If the other side has a point, learn from them. If they're wrong, rebut them. Teach them. Beat them on the battlefield of ideas. And you might as well start practising now, because one thing I can guarantee you – you will have to deal with ignorance, hatred, racism, foolishness, trifling folks. I promise you, you will have to deal with all that at every stage of your life. That may not seem fair, but life has never been

So don't try to shut folks out, don't try to shut them down, no matter how much you might disagree with them.

completely fair. Nobody promised you a crystal stair. And if you want to make life fair, then you've got to start with the world as it is.

So that's my advice. That's how you change things. Change isn't something that happens every four years or eight years; change is not placing your faith in any particular politician and then just putting your feet up and saying, OK, go. Change is the effort of committed citizens who hitch their wagons to something bigger than themselves and fight for it every single day.

That's what Thurgood Marshall understood – a man who once walked this year, graduated from Howard Law; went home to Baltimore, started his own law practice. He and his mentor, Charles Hamilton Houston, rolled up their sleeves and they set out to overturn segregation. They worked through the NAACP. Filed dozens of lawsuits, fought dozens of cases. And after nearly 20 years of effort – 20 years – Thurgood Marshall ultimately succeeded in bringing his righteous cause before the Supreme Court, and securing the ruling in Brown v. Board of Education that separate could never be equal. Twenty years.

Marshall, Houston – they knew it would not be easy. They knew it would not be quick. They knew all sorts of obstacles would stand in their way. They knew that even if they won, that would just be the beginning of a longer march to equality. But they had discipline. They had persistence. They had faith – and a sense of humour. And they made life better for all Americans.

And I know you graduates share those qualities. I know it because I've learned about some of the young people graduating here today. There's a young woman named Ciearra Jefferson, who's graduating with you. And I'm just going to use her as an example. I hope you don't mind, Ciearra. Ciearra grew up in Detroit and was raised by a poor single mom who worked seven days a week in an auto plant. And for a time, her family found themselves without a place to call home. They bounced around between friends and family who might take them in. By her senior year, Ciearra was up at 5am every day, juggling homework, extracurricular activities, volunteering, all while taking care of her little sister. But she knew that education was her ticket to a better life. So she never gave up. Pushed herself to excel. This daughter of a single mom who works on the assembly line turned down a full scholarship to Harvard to come to Howard.

And today, like many of you, Ciearra is the first in her family to graduate from college. And then, she says, she's going to go back to her hometown, just like Thurgood Marshall did, to make sure all the working folks she grew up with have access to the health care they need and deserve. As she puts it, she's going to be a 'change agent'. She's going to reach back and help folks like her succeed.

And people like Ciearra are why I remain optimistic about America. Young people like you are why I never give in to despair.

James Baldwin once wrote, 'Not everything that is faced can be changed, but nothing can be changed until it is faced.'

Graduates, each of us is only here because someone else faced down challenges for us. We are only who we are because someone else struggled and sacrificed for us. That's not just Thurgood Marshall's story, or Ciearra's story, or my story, or your story – that is the story of America. A story whispered by slaves in the cotton fields, the song of marchers in Selma, the dream of a King in the shadow of Lincoln. The prayer of immigrants who set out for a new world. The roar of women demanding the vote. The rallying cry of workers who built America. And the GIs who bled overseas for our freedom.

Now it's your turn. And the good news is, you're ready. And when your journey seems too hard, and when you run into a chorus of cynics who tell you that you're being foolish to keep believing or that you can't do something, or that you should just give up, or you should just settle – you might say to yourself a little phrase that I've found handy these last eight years: yes, we can.

Congratulations, Class of 2016! Good luck! God bless you. God bless the United States of America. I'm proud of you.

IAN MCEWAN

ON FREE SPEECH

Dickinson College, 2015

My most sincere congratulations to all the graduates here. You made it through. You have a degree from a truly excellent institution. A lot of reading, writing, lying in bed (thinking, of course). And now you stand on one of life's various summits. As you know, there's only one way off a summit – but that's another story. Don't be taken in by those who tell you that life is short. It's inordinately long. I was into my twenties when my mother astonished me by saying wistfully, 'I'd give anything to be forty-five again.' Forty-five sounded like old age to me then. Now I see what she meant. Most of you have more than 20 years before you peak. Barring all-out nuclear war or a catastrophic meteor collision, a substantial minority of you will get a toe in the door of the next century – a very wrinkled, arthritic toe, but the same toe you're wearing now. You have a lot of years in the bank – but don't worry, I'm not here to tell you how to spend them.

Instead, I would like to share a few thoughts with you about free speech (and speech here includes writing and reading, listening and thinking) – free speech – the

Let's begin on a positive note: there is likely more free speech, free thought, free enquiry on earth now than at any previous moment in recorded history.

life blood, the essential condition of the liberal education you've just received. Let's begin on a positive note:
there is likely more free speech, free thought, free enquiry
on earth now than at any previous moment in recorded
history (even taking into account the golden age of the
so-called 'pagan' philosophers). And you've come of age
in a country where the enshrinement of free speech in the
First Amendment is not an empty phrase, as it is in many
constitutions, but a living reality.

But free speech was, it is and always will be, under
attack – from the political right, the left, the centre. It will
come from under your feet, from the extremes of religion
as well as from unreligious ideologies. It's never conveni-
ent, especially for entrenched power, to have a lot of free
speech flying around.

The words associated with Voltaire (more likely, his
sentiments but not his actual phrasing) remain crucial
and should never be forgotten: I disapprove of what you
say, but I will defend to the death your right to say it. It's
only rarely appropriate to suppress the speech of those
you disagree with. As my late friend Christopher Hitchens
used to say, when you meet a flat-earther or a creation-
ist, it can be useful to be made to remember just why
you think the earth is round or whether you're capable
of making the case for natural selection. For that reason,
it's a poor principle, adopted in some civilized countries,

to imprison the deniers of the Holocaust or the Armenian massacres, however contemptible they might be.

It's worth remembering this: freedom of expression sustains all the other freedoms we enjoy. Without free speech, democracy is a sham. Every freedom we possess or wish to possess (of habeas corpus and due process, of universal franchise and of assembly, union representation, sexual equality, of sexual preference, of the rights of children, of animals – the list goes on) has had to be freely thought and talked and written into existence. No single individual can generate these rights alone. The process is cumulative. It was a historical context of relative freedom of speech that made possible the work of those who were determined to extend that liberty. John Milton, Tom Paine, Mary Wollstonecraft, George Washington, Thomas Jefferson, John Stuart Mill, Oliver Wendell Holmes – the roll call is long and honourable – and that is why an education in the liberal arts is so vital to the culture you are about to contribute to.

Take a long journey from these shores as I'm sure many of you will, and you will find the condition of free expression to be desperate. Across almost the entire Middle East, free thought can bring punishment or death, from governments or from street mobs or motivated individuals. The same is true in Bangladesh, Pakistan, across great swathes of Africa. These past years the public space for free thought in Russia has been shrinking. In China, state monitoring of free expression is on an industrial scale. To censor daily the Internet alone, the Chinese government employs as many as fifty thousand bureaucrats – a level of thought repression unprecedented in human history.

Paradoxically, it's all the more important to be vigilant for free expression wherever it flourishes. And nowhere has it been more jealously guarded than under the First Amendment of the US Constitution. Which is why it has been so puzzling lately, when we saw scores of American writers publicly disassociating themselves from a PEN gala to honour the murdered journalists of the French satirical magazine, *Charlie Hebdo*. American PEN exists to defend and promote free speech. What a disappointment that so many American authors could not stand with courageous fellow writers and artists at a time of tragedy. The magazine has been scathing about racism. It's also scathing about organized religion and politicians and it might not be to your taste – but that's when you should remember your Voltaire.

Hebdo's offices were fire-bombed in 2011, and the journalists kept going. They received constant death threats – and they kept going. In January nine colleagues were murdered, gunned down, in their office – the editorial staff kept going and within days they had produced an edition whose cover forgave their attackers. TOUT EST PARDONNE, all is forgiven. All this, when in the US and

UK one threatening phone call can be enough to stop a major publishing house in its tracks.

The attack on *Charlie Hebdo* came from religious fanatics whose allegiances became clear when one of the accomplices made her way from France, through Turkey to ISIS in Syria. Remember, this is a form of fanaticism whose victims, across Africa and the Middle East, are mostly Muslims – Muslim gays and feminists, Muslim reformists, bloggers, human rights activists, dissidents, apostates, novelists and ordinary citizens, including children, murdered in or kidnapped from their schools.

There's a phenomenon in intellectual life that I call bi-polar thinking. Let's not side with *Charlie Hebdo* because it might seem as if we're endorsing George Bush's 'war on terror'. This is a suffocating form of intellectual tribalism and a poor way of thinking for yourself. As a German novelist friend wrote to me in anguish about the PEN affair – 'It's the Seventies again: Let's not support the Russian dissidents, because it would get "applause from the wrong side."' That terrible phrase.

But note the end of the *Hebdo* affair: the gala went ahead, the surviving journalists received a thunderous and prolonged standing ovation from American PEN.

Timothy Garton Ash reminds us in a new book on free speech that 'The U.S. Supreme Court has described academic freedom as a "special concern of the First Amendment."' Worrying too, then, is the case of Ayaan

Hirsi Ali, an ex Muslim, highly critical of Islam, too critical for some. As a victim herself, she has campaigned against female genital mutilation. She has campaigned for the rights of Muslim women. In a recent book she has argued that for Islam to live more at ease in the modern world it needs to rethink its attitudes to homosexuality, to the interpretation of the Koran as the literal word of God, to blasphemy, to punishing severely those who want to leave the religion. Contrary to what some have suggested, such arguments are neither racist nor driven by hatred. But she has received death threats. Crucially, on many American campuses she is not welcomed, and, notoriously, Brandeis withdrew its offer of an honorary degree. Islam is worthy of respect, as indeed is atheism. We want respect flowing in all directions. But religion and atheism, and all thought systems, all grand claims to truth, must be open to criticism, satire, even, sometimes, mockery. Surely, we have not forgotten the lessons of the Salman Rushdie affair.

Campus intolerance of inconvenient speakers is hardly new. Back in the sixties my own university blocked a psychologist for promoting the idea of a hereditable component to intelligence. In the seventies, the great American biologist E.O. Wilson was drowned out for suggesting a genetic element in human social behaviour. As I remember, both men were called fascists. The ideas of these men did not fit prevailing ideologies, but their views are unexceptionable today.

More broadly – the Internet has, of course, provided extraordinary possibilities for free speech. At the same time, it has taken us on to some difficult and unexpected terrain. It has led to the slow decline of local newspapers, and so removed a sceptical and knowledgeable voice from local politics. Privacy is an essential element of free expression; the Snowden files have revealed an extraordinary and unnecessary level of email surveillance by government agencies. Another essential element of free expression is access to information; the Internet has concentrated huge power over that access into the hands of private companies like Google, Facebook and Twitter. We need to be careful that such power is not abused. Large pharmaceutical companies have been known to withhold research information vital to the public interest. On another scale, the death of young black men in police custody could be framed as the ultimate sanction against free expression. As indeed is poverty and poor educational resources.

All these issues need the input of men and women with a liberal arts education and you, graduates, are well placed to form your own conclusions. And you may reasonably conclude that free speech is not simple. It's never an absolute. We don't give space to proselytizing paedophiles, to racists (and remember, race is not identical to religion) or to those who wish to incite violence against others. Wendell Holmes's hypothetical 'shouting fire in a crowded theatre' is still relevant. But it can be a little too easy sometimes to dismiss arguments you don't like as 'hate speech' or to complain that this or that speaker makes you feel 'disrespected'. Being offended is not to be confused with a state of grace; it's the occasional price we all pay for living in an open society. Being robust is no bad thing. Either engage, with arguments – not with banishments and certainly not with guns – or, as an American Muslim teacher said recently at Friday prayers, ignore the entire matter.

In making your mind up on these issues, I hope you'll remember your time at Dickinson and the novels you may have read here. It would prompt you, I hope, in the direction of mental freedom. The novel as a literary form was born out of the Enlightenment, out of curiosity about and respect for the individual. Its traditions impel it towards pluralism, openness, a sympathetic desire to inhabit the minds of others. There is no man, woman or child, on earth whose mind the novel cannot reconstruct. Totalitarian systems are right with regard to their narrow interests when they lock up novelists. The novel is, or can be, the ultimate expression of free speech.

I hope you'll use your fine liberal education to preserve for future generations the beautiful and precious but also awkward, sometimes inconvenient and even offensive culture of freedom of expression we have. Take with you these celebrated words of George Washington: 'If the freedom of speech is taken away then, dumb and silent, we may be led like sheep to the slaughter.'

We may be certain that Dickinson has not prepared you to be sheep. Good luck 2015 graduates in whatever you choose to do in life.

GLORIA STEINEM

GO THE DISTANCE

Smith College, 2007

To the beloved, brave, tired and now headed-for-the-world graduates of the Class of 2007; the first generation of Facebook and YouTube Smithies; the class to shape and survive the most changes in the way Smith lives; the second class of the Iraq War; and the most diverse class in the history of Smith College, from Adas* – who made sure that Class (economic class) Is Never Dismissed – and to all those who help Smith College look more like the world: I thank you for including me in your historic day.

It's historic for me, too, because I was sitting where you sit today exactly 51 years ago. I wasn't sure I should bring up this half-century fact. For one thing, I feel connected to you, not distant. For another, I feared you might go into as much age shock as I did when I woke up after my seventieth birthday, and thought, There's a 70-year-old woman in my bed! How did this happen?!

* 'Adas' are Ada Comstock scholars, students enrolled in a Smith College programme that enables women of nontraditional college age to complete a Bachelor of Arts degree at a realistic pace.

But then I realized that fearing separation by age was probably more my generation's problem than yours.

If I conjure up my own graduation day, for instance, even life after 30 seemed a hazy screen to be filled in by the needs of others – and there were not yet even Adas to show us that life and growth continue. In our age ghetto, we pretty much accepted the idea that women were more valued for giving birth to others than for giving birth to ourselves. Yes, many of us had professions, but they were secondary. As one of my classmates said in the light of later feminism, 'I didn't have a job, I had a jobette.' We weren't trying to change the world to fit women – and neither was Smith in those days – we were trying to change ourselves to fit the world.

If this seems hard to believe now, think of my two most famous age peers: Marilyn Monroe, who literally feared ageing more than death, and Smith's own Sylvia Plath, whose world-class talent couldn't give her the autonomy she needed to survive.

Now, thanks to decades of feminist rebellion, your generation is much more likely to value minds and hearts and talents that last just as long as you do. You have not only a somewhat longer life expectancy physically, but faith in a much longer life of your own making. Fortunately for me, this also means you are better able to identify with other women across boundaries of age. The end doesn't justify the means; the means are the ends. For instance: my generation of young women said things like, 'I'm not going to be anything like my mother.' After all, if we didn't blame our mothers for living vicarious lives, we would have to admit that we might have to do the same thing.

Even now, my generation – and probably some of yours, too – are living out the unlived lives of our mothers. This is honourable and rewarding and loving, but it isn't the same – for either mother or daughter – as living our own unique lives.

Now, I meet many young women who say something like, 'I hope I can have as interesting a life as my mother.' Not the same life, but as interesting. And when I hear this, it brings tears to my eyes – because I know there is not only love between generations, as there always has been, but now there is respect, learning, a sense of balance, even an invitation to adventure and freedom.

So instead of worrying about the decades between us, I thought I would use them as a measure of tomorrow by projecting a similar time into the future. Like the swing of a compass arm, I invite you to measure the progress made in the time between my graduating class and yours, and project into the future the same distance. What might the world be like when you come back to visit the Class of 2057? I'm not suggesting we know what will happen, but I am suggesting that imagining is a form of planning.

So let's take a concrete example: in my generation, we were asked by the Smith vocational office how many

There is not only love between generations ... there is respect, learning, a sense of balance, even an invitation to adventure and freedom.

words we could type a minute, a question that was never asked of then all-male students at Harvard or Princeton. Female-only typing was rationalized by supposedly greater female verbal skills, attention to detail, smaller fingers, goodness knows what, but the public imagination just didn't include male typists – certainly not Ivy League-educated ones. Now, computers have come along, and 'typing' is 'keyboarding'. Suddenly, voila! – men can type! Gives you faith in men's ability to change, doesn't it?

So maybe by 2057, occupational segregation – an even greater cause of wage disparity than unequal pay for the same job – may have changed enough so there will be male nurses and female surgeons. Then male medics won't come home from the military to be shamed out of good nursing jobs, and nursing will be better paid because it will no longer be a pink-collar ghetto. Also perhaps parking-lot attendants will no longer be paid more than childcare attendants – as is now the case not because we value our cars more than our children, but because the first are almost totally male and the second are almost totally female. And most of all, maybe the vast unpaid area of caregiving – whether that means raising children or caring for the ill and elderly, it is at least 30 per cent of the productive work in this country and more than half in many countries – maybe this huge and vital area of work will at last have an attributed economic value, whether it is done by women or men.

This is already a feminist proposal for tax policy. It would mean the attributed value of caregiving would become tax deductible for those who pay taxes, and tax refundable for those who are too poor to pay taxes, thus substituting for the disaster of welfare. It would be a huge advance. We would at last be valuing all productive work, including that mysteriously defined as not-work – as in homemakers who 'don't work', even though they work longer and harder than any other class of worker. (Not to mention with more likelihood of getting replaced by a younger worker.)

Take something deeper: my generation identified emotionally with every other vulnerable group, but without understanding why. Fifty years later, we understand why: females are an 'out' group, too – no wonder we identified. Now, there are local, national and global liberation movements based on sex, race, ethnicity, sexuality and class. We know that in these movements we are each other's allies, if only because our adversaries are all the same.

Perhaps fifty years from now, the public imagination will finally understand that this is one inseparable movement. The same hierarchy that controls women's bodies as the means of reproduction – which is how we women got into this jam in the first place – and the same one that says that sexuality is only moral when it is directed towards reproduction within patriarchal marriage, also controls reproduction in order to maintain racial difference and to preserve a racist caste system. Then, we will understand better that it's impossible to be a feminist without also being an antiracist – and vice versa. Not only because women are in every group in the world, but because racial caste and sexual caste are intertwined, interdependent and inseparable.

We will also understand that the same folks who are against contraception and abortion and even the sex education that helps avoid abortion – anything that allows the separation of sexuality from reproduction – are also against sexual expression between two women or between two men. They deny the reality that human sexuality has always been a form of communication and pleasure, not just a way we reproduce. (And I do mean always. The Native women who lived on this very land long before Europeans showed up often had two or three children two or three years apart. They absolutely understood contraception and abortifacients. This is not just some modern gift from the pharmaceutical industry, though it was Margaret Sanger who financed and encouraged such research.)

No wonder anti-equality, racist and antigay forces are all the same, just as they were in, say, Germany under fascism, or in theocracies and totalitarian regimes now. Perhaps 50 years from now, most people will understand that reproductive and sexual freedom – and democratic families, democracy within families – are as necessary to democracy as is the vote and freedom of speech.

Or take another area very close to home. My generation often accepted the idea that the private/public roles of women and men were 'natural'. Your generation has made giant strides into public life, but often still says: how can I combine career and family? I say to you from the bottom of my heart that when you ask that question you are setting your sights way too low.

First of all, there can be no answer until men are asking the same question. Second, every other modern democracy in the world is way, way ahead of this country in providing a national system of childcare and job patterns adapted to the needs of parents, both men and women. So don't get guilty. Get mad. Get active.

If this is a problem that affects millions of unique women, then the only answer is to organize together. I know it may be hard for women to believe that men can be loving and nurturing of small children – just as it may be hard for men to believe that women can be as expert and achieving in public life. If you've never seen a deer, it's hard to see a deer. If I hadn't happened to have a father who raised me as a small child as much as my mother did, I might not believe it either.

But raising young children – or being raised to raise children – is the way men are most likely to develop their own full circle of human qualities, and to stop reproducing the prison of the 'masculine' role, just as our role in the public life frees us of the prison of the 'feminine' role.

For that matter, our kids do what they see, not what they are told. If children don't see whole people, they're much less likely to become whole people – at least, not without a lot of hard work in later life.

Which leads us into the big question of violence. Gender roles provide the slippery slope to the normalization of control and violence in all their forms, from sexualized violence to military violence – which is the distance from A to B. Until the family paradigm of human relationships is about cooperation and not domination or hierarchy, we're unlikely to imagine cooperation as normal or even possible in public life.

We must change this paradigm. It is just too dangerous in this era of weapons – especially as it collides with religions that extol Doomsday. It's already too dangerous in this era when there are more slaves in proportion to the world's population – more people held by force or coercion without benefit from their work – than there were in the 1800s.

Sex trafficking, labour trafficking, children and adults forced into armies: they all add up to a global human-trafficking industry that is more profitable than the arms trade, and second only to the drug trade. The big difference now from the 1800s is that the United Nations estimates that 80 per cent of those who are enslaved are women and children. Yes, all this will take much longer than our projected 50 years to transform.

Make sure you meet
with a few friends
once a week or once
a month, people you
can share
experiences and
hopes with – and
vice versa.

The wisdom of original cultures tells us that it takes four generations to heal one violent act. But it's also true that, if we were to raise even one generation of children without violence and without shaming, we have no idea what might be possible.

It won't be easy to hang on to this vision of possibilities in ourselves and in others if we are alone in a world that's organized a different way. We are communal creatures. So make sure you're not alone after you leave this community at Smith. Make sure you meet with a few friends once a week or once a month, people you can share experiences and hopes with – and vice versa. Women may need this even more than other marginalized groups because, after all, we will never have our own country (good thing – it makes us antinationalistic); we don't have a neighbourhood; most of us don't even have a bar.

If I had one wish for women worldwide, it would be a kind of global version of Alcoholics Anonymous: a network of women's groups – also welcoming to men who have the same radical vision. These leaderless and free groups would exist in cities and villages, in school basements and around rural wells. They could spread like lace over the globe and their purpose would be to support self-authority. After all, democracy can't exist without the female half of the world's population.

While we're at it over the next 50 years, remember that the end doesn't justify the means; the means are the ends. If we want joy and music and friendship and laughter at the end of our revolution, we must have joy and music and friendship and laughter along the way. Emma Goldman had the right idea about dancing at the revolution.

So, my beloved comrades, yes this is the longest of all revolutions and that will mean a lot of struggle, a lot of organizing together and a lot of unity, but that also means a lot of dancing.

For now, just measure the distance from my graduation to yours – from my class with only one student of colour to your diverse class, from my era of no women's history to yours that has been strengthened by women's history. You will see that you can match or surpass that distance that we have covered.

Now, it's true that I have every intention of living to be a hundred. But even I, hope-oholic that I am, know that when you return to celebrate your victories and inspire the Class of 2057, I won't be with you. But then again: I will.

NEIL GAIMAN

MAKE GOOD ART

University of the Arts, 2012

never really expected to find myself giving advice to people graduating from an establishment of higher education. I never graduated from any such establishment. I never even started at one. I escaped from school as soon as I could, when the prospect of four more years of enforced learning before I'd become the writer I wanted to be was stifling.

I got out into the world, I wrote, and I became a better writer the more I wrote, and I wrote some more, and nobody ever seemed to mind that I was making it up as I went along, they just read what I wrote and they paid for it, or they didn't, and often they commissioned me to write something else for them.

Which has left me with a healthy respect and fondness for higher education that those of my friends and family, who attended universities, were cured of long ago.

Looking back, I've had a remarkable ride. I'm not sure I can call it a career, because a career implies that I had some kind of career plan, and I never did. The nearest thing I had was a list I made when I was 15 of everything I wanted to do: to write an adult novel, a children's book, a comic, a movie, record an audiobook, write an episode of *Doctor Who* ... and so on. I didn't have a career. I just did the next thing on the list.

So I thought I'd tell you everything I wish I'd known starting out, and a few things that, looking back on it, I suppose that I did know. And that I would also give you the best piece of advice I'd ever got, which I completely failed to follow.

First of all: when you start out on a career in the arts you have no idea what you are doing.

This is great. People who know what they are doing know the rules, and know what is possible and impossible. You do not. And you should not. The rules on what is possible and impossible in the arts were made by people who had not tested the bounds of the possible by going beyond them. And you can.

If you don't know it's impossible it's easier to do. And because nobody's done it before, they haven't made up rules to stop anyone doing that again, yet.

Secondly, if you have an idea of what you want to make, what you were put here to do, then just go and do that.

And that's much harder than it sounds and, sometimes in the end, so much easier than you might imagine. Because normally, there are things you have to do before you can get to the place you want to be. I wanted to write comics and novels and stories and films, so I became a journalist, because journalists are allowed to ask questions, and to simply go and find out how the world works, and besides, to do those things I needed to write and to write well, and I was being paid to learn how to write economically, crisply, sometimes under adverse conditions, and on time.

Sometimes the way to do what you hope to do will be clear cut, and sometimes it will be almost impossible to decide whether or not you are doing the correct thing, because you'll have to balance your goals and hopes with feeding yourself, paying debts, finding work, settling for what you can get.

Something that worked for me was imagining that where I wanted to be – an author, primarily of fiction, making good books, making good comics and supporting myself through my words – was a mountain. A distant mountain. My goal.

And I knew that as long as I kept walking towards the mountain I would be all right. And when I truly was not sure what to do, I could stop, and think about whether it was taking me towards or away from the mountain. I said no to editorial jobs on magazines, proper jobs that would have paid proper money because I knew that, attractive though they were, for me they would have been walking away from the mountain. And if those job offers had come along earlier I might have taken them, because they still would have been closer to the mountain than I was at the time.

I learned to write by writing. I tended to do anything as long as it felt like an adventure, and to stop when it felt like work, which meant that life did not feel like work.

Thirdly, when you start off, you have to deal with the problems of failure. You need to be thick-skinned, to learn that not every project will survive. A freelance life, a life in the arts, is sometimes like putting messages in bottles, on a desert island, and hoping that someone will find one of your bottles and open it and read it, and put something in a bottle that will wash its way back to you: appreciation, or a commission, or money, or love. And you have to accept that you may put out a hundred things for every bottle that winds up coming back.

The problems of failure are problems of discouragement, of hopelessness, of hunger. You want everything to happen and you want it now, and things go wrong. My first book – a piece of journalism I had done for the money, and which had already bought me an electric typewriter from the advance – should have been a bestseller. It should have paid me a lot of money. If the publisher hadn't gone into involuntary liquidation between the first print run selling out and the second printing, and before any royalties could be paid, it would have done.

And I shrugged, and I still had my electric typewriter and enough money to pay the rent for a couple of months, and I decided that I would do my best in future not to write books just for the money. If you didn't get the money, then you didn't have anything. If I did work I was proud of, and I didn't get the money, at least I'd have the work.

Every now and again, I forget that rule, and whenever I do, the universe kicks me hard and reminds me. I don't know that it's an issue for anybody but me, but it's true that nothing I did where the only reason for doing it was the money was ever worth it, except as bitter experience. Usually I didn't wind up getting the money, either. The things I did because I was excited, and wanted to see them exist in reality have never let me down, and I've never regretted the time I spent on any of them.

The problems of failure are hard.

The problems of success can be harder, because nobody warns you about them.

The first problem of any kind of even limited success is the unshakable conviction that you are getting away with something, and that any moment now they will discover you. It's Imposter Syndrome, something my wife Amanda christened the Fraud Police.

In my case, I was convinced that there would be a knock on the door, and a man with a clipboard (I don't know why he carried a clipboard, in my head, but he did) would be there, to tell me it was all over, and they had caught up with me, and now I would have to go and get a real job, one that didn't consist of making things up and writing them down, and reading books I wanted to read. And then I would go away quietly and get the kind of job where you don't have to make things up any more.

I hope you'll make mistakes. If you're making mistakes, it means you're out there doing something. And the mistakes in themselves can be useful.

The problems of success. They're real, and with luck you'll experience them. The point where you stop saying yes to everything, because now the bottles you threw in the ocean are all coming back, and have to learn to say no.

I watched my peers, and my friends, and the ones who were older than me and watched how miserable some of them were: I'd listen to them telling me that they couldn't envisage a world where they did what they had always wanted to do any more, because now they had to earn a certain amount every month just to keep where they were. They couldn't go and do the things that mattered, and that they had really wanted to do; and that seemed as big a tragedy as any problem of failure.

And after that, the biggest problem of success is that the world conspires to stop you doing the thing that you do, because you are successful. There was a day when I looked up and realized that I had become someone who professionally replied to email, and who wrote as a hobby. I started answering fewer emails, and was relieved to find I was writing much more.

Fourthly, I hope you'll make mistakes. If you're making mistakes, it means you're out there doing something. And the mistakes in themselves can be useful. I once misspelled Caroline, in a letter, transposing the A and the O, and I thought, '*Coraline* looks like a real name ...'

And remember that whatever discipline you are in, whether you are a musician or a photographer, a fine artist or a cartoonist, a writer, a dancer, a designer, whatever you do you have one thing that's unique. You have the ability to make art.

And for me, and for so many of the people I have known, that's been a lifesaver. The ultimate lifesaver. It gets you through good times and it gets you through the other ones.

Life is sometimes hard. Things go wrong, in life and in love and in business and in friendship and in health and in all the other ways that life can go wrong. And when things get tough, this is what you should do.

Make good art.

I'm serious. Husband runs off with a politician? Make good art. Leg crushed and then eaten by mutated boa constrictor? Make good art. IRS on your trail? Make good art. Cat exploded? Make good art. Somebody on the Internet thinks what you do is stupid or evil or it's all been done before? Make good art. Probably things will work out somehow, and eventually time will take the sting away, but that doesn't matter. Do what only you do best. Make good art.

Make it on the good days too.

And fifthly, while you are at it, make *your* art. Do the stuff that only you can do.

The urge, starting out, is to copy. And that's not a bad thing. Most of us only find our own voices after we've sounded like a lot of other people. But the one thing that you have that nobody else has is *you*. Your voice, your mind, your story, your vision. So write and draw and build and play and dance and live as only you can.

The moment that you feel that, just possibly, you're walking down the street naked, exposing too much of your heart and your mind and what exists on the inside, showing too much of yourself. That's the moment you may be starting to get it right.

The things I've done that worked the best were the things I was the least certain about, the stories where I was sure they would either work, or more likely be the kinds of embarrassing failures people would gather together and talk about until the end of time. They always had that in common: looking back at them, people explain why they were inevitable successes. While I was doing them, I had no idea.

I still don't. And where would be the fun in making something you knew was going to work?

And sometimes the things I did really didn't work. There are stories of mine that have never been reprinted. Some of them never even left the house. But I learned as much from them as I did from the things that worked.

Sixthly. I will pass on some secret freelancer knowledge. Secret knowledge is always good. And it is useful for anyone who ever plans to create art for other people, to enter a freelance world of any kind. I learned it in comics, but it applies to other fields too. And it's this:

People get hired because, somehow, they get hired. In my case I did something which these days would be easy to check, and would get me into trouble, and when I started out, in those pre-Internet days, seemed like a sensible career strategy: when I was asked by editors who I'd worked for, I lied. I listed a handful of magazines that sounded likely, and I sounded confident, and I got jobs. I then made it a point of honour to have written something for each of the magazines I'd listed to get that first job, so that I hadn't actually lied, I'd just been chronologically challenged ... You get work however you get work.

People keep working, in a freelance world, and more and more of today's world is freelance, because their work is good, and because they are easy to get along with, and because they deliver the work on time. And you don't even need all three. Two out of three is fine. People will tolerate how unpleasant you are if your work is good and you deliver it on time. They'll forgive the lateness of the work if it's good, and if they like you. And you don't have to be as good as the others if you're on time and it's always a pleasure to hear from you.

When I agreed to give this address, I started trying to think what the best advice I'd been given over the years was.

And it came from Stephen King 20 years ago, at the height of the success of *Sandman*. I was writing a comic that people loved and were taking seriously. King had liked *Sandman* and my novel with Terry Pratchett, *Good Omens*, and he saw the madness, the long signing lines, all that, and his advice was this:

'*This is really great. You should enjoy it.*'

And I didn't. Best advice I got that I ignored. Instead I worried about it. I worried about the next deadline, the next idea, the next story. There wasn't a moment for the next 14 or 15 years that I wasn't writing something in my head, or wondering about it. And I didn't stop and look around and go, *this is really fun.* I wish I'd enjoyed it more. It's been an amazing ride. But there were parts of the ride I missed, because I was too worried about things going wrong, about what came next, to enjoy the bit I was on.

That was the hardest lesson for me, I think: to let go and enjoy the ride, because the ride takes you to some remarkable and unexpected places.

And here, on this platform, today, is one of those places. (I am enjoying myself immensely.)

To all today's graduates: I wish you luck. Luck is useful. Often you will discover that the harder you work, and the more wisely you work, the luckier you get. But there is luck, and it helps.

We're in a transitional world right now, if you're in any kind of artistic field, because the nature of distribution is changing, the models by which creators got their work out into the world, and got to keep a roof over their heads and buy sandwiches while they did that, are all changing. I've talked to people at the top of the food chain in publishing, in bookselling, in all those areas, and nobody knows what

Often you will discover that the harder you work, and the more wisely you work, the luckier you get. But there is luck, and it helps.

the landscape will look like two years from now, let alone a decade away. The distribution channels that people had built over the last century or so are in flux for print, for visual artists, for musicians, for creative people of all kinds.

Which is, on the one hand, intimidating, and on the other, immensely liberating. The rules, the assumptions, the now-we're-supposed-tos of how you get your work seen, and what you do then, are breaking down. The gate-keepers are leaving their gates. You can be as creative as you need to be to get your work seen. YouTube and the Web (and whatever comes after YouTube and the Web) can give you more people watching than television ever did. The old rules are crumbling and nobody knows what the new rules are.

So make up your own rules.

Someone asked me recently how to do something she thought was going to be difficult, in this case recording an audio book, and I suggested she pretend that she was someone who could do it. Not pretend to do it, but pretend she was someone who could. She put up a notice to this effect on the studio wall, and she said it helped.

So be wise, because the world needs more wisdom, and if you cannot be wise, pretend to be someone who is wise, and then just behave like they would.

And now go, and make interesting mistakes, make amazing mistakes, make glorious and fantastic mistakes. Break rules. Leave the world more interesting for your being here. Make good art.

CREDITS